# Fight Like A Girl

Michael G. Lewis

Illustrations by: Hila Ronis

Fitzroy Books

Published by Fitzroy Books
An imprint of
Regal House Publishing, LLC
Raleigh, NC 27612
All rights reserved

https://fitzroybooks.com

Printed in the United States of America

ISBN -13: 9781646030019
Library of Congress Control Number: 2021932392

Interior and cover design by Lafayette & Greene
Cover and interior images © by Hila Ronis

Regal House Publishing, LLC
https://regalhousepublishing.com

This book is dedicated to women warriors everywhere, whose contributions to history—and our own lives personally—have gone unappreciated for too long. Whether you're on the battlefield or in the boardroom, raising kids or curing cancer, running marathons or running countries, patrolling the streets or pushing for justice, the world owes you a colossal debt of gratitude—thank you.

# Author's Note

When I was growing up, gender roles were very clearly defined. The girls we played with never joined the boys when we were "playing army" because, well, girls weren't soldiers. Any mention of women relating to war usually conjured up images of nurses or, perhaps, someone involved in behind-the-scenes press corps or administrative duties. But not actual fighting. That was for the boys.

How wrong we were.

While researching eighteenth-century pirates Anne Bonny and Mary Read for a project, I stumbled across a treasure trove of fascinating stories about women in combat through the ages. Their stories were powerful, inspirational, and amazing.

While *Fight Like A Girl* is a mere snapshot of only twenty-five female warriors, we could easily add several zeroes to that number. Women have been successfully fighting in combat roles since the beginning of time. During my research, I discovered women warriors in nearly every century, country, and culture. Their differences are many—some were queens, some prostitutes, some fought for country, others for religion, while others were motivated by blind loyalty, bloodlust, fame, revenge, and even plain old fashioned greed. Yes, their differences are many, but they are more defined by striking similarities— all were smart, stubborn, almost supernaturally brave, and extraordinary.

Their stories are inspiring but also chilling, their exploits tragic, triumphant, awe inspiring, and even humorous. They're also relatively unknown, which is why it's both baffling and infuriating that their tales have all but found a sad home in the proverbial dustbin of history. These women warriors—these "Band of Sisters,"as it were—had far-reaching effects on the entire world, since some of their exploits literally changed the course of history.

Their stories deserve to be told.

*Michael G. Lewis*

# Deborah Sampson

*Why can I not fight for my country too?*

Cleaning the nasty sword wound on the soldier's forehead was the easy part, but there were still two musket balls embedded in his thigh and time was of the essence. If the bullets weren't extracted and treated immediately, the doctor knew that infection was sure to set in, resulting in the likely amputation of his leg. The battle outside Tarrytown, New York, had resulted in a significant number of casualties for the colonialists fighting against the British in 1776, and the hospital field tent was filled with the groans of wounded and dying soldiers. To make matters worse, the soldier with the bullets in his leg refused to let the doctor cut away his clothes so the wounds could be treated.

"I can take care of this myself!" the soldier insisted.

"If you don't let me treat those wounds, you'll lose your leg and probably your life!" the doctor explained again, running out of patience. "And if we spend any more time arguing about this, other soldiers here will die as well!"

Reluctantly, the wounded soldier lay back on the operating table. "Go ahead," he said. The doctor turned away to reach for his instruments, but when he looked back seconds later, the soldier was gone.

It was only years later, after the Revolutionary War had ended, that the kind doctor learned he hadn't been operating on a soldier named Robert Shurtliff, after all, but a female soldier by the name of Deborah Sampson who had escaped the field hospital that day seconds before her true identity was discovered.

Though Sampson's early life was fraught with difficulty, nothing could have prepared her for the horrors she witnessed during her time as a soldier. Her father abandoned his family when Deborah was a young girl, leaving her mother and six other siblings destitute. Deborah was sent to live with relatives but became, in subsequent years, an indentured servant on a farm in Massachusetts. During this time, she educated herself, learning to read and write, while developing other valuable skills such as baking, carpentry, and woodworking. Though the hours were long and the work often difficult, Deborah soon developed into a tall and extraordinarily strong young woman. She was released from servitude on her eighteenth birthday and left the farm to pursue a career as a school teacher. She enjoyed teaching, but the Revolutionary War soon raged around her and she witnessed many of her male friends, former students, and family members join the colonial forces to fight the British. Deborah felt compelled to do her part, though in a most unconventional way—she decided to disguise herself as a man and join George Washington's Continental Army as a fighting soldier.

It was a risky move—and more than a little brazen—but as implausible as it may seem now, it wasn't all that difficult back then for someone like Deborah to pull it off. She was taller and stronger than most men at the time, and she could easily conceal her small breasts by binding them with linen cloth and wearing loose clothing.

Sampson's first attempt to enlist failed when she was recognized by someone she knew as she was signing up. She was tossed out of the army, forced to repay her enlistment bonus, and shunned by several friends, neighbors, and members of her church. Sampson was discouraged but not deterred. She traveled to upstate New York where no one knew her and enlisted again under the moniker Robert Shurtliff. This second attempt was successful and she found herself on the training ground with her fellow volunteers.

Sampson possessed superior skills as a soldier and was soon assigned to Captain George Webb's Company of Light Infantry, an elite unit comprised of soldiers known for their size, strength, and bravery in combat. As her battlefield experiences broadened, Sampson sharpened her extraordinary skills. Sampson embarked on a series of dangerous scouting missions and excursions. During one raid, she led a group of thirty men against a Tory stronghold, capturing fifteen of the enemy. At the Siege of Yorktown, she dug trenches under heavy cannon fire, and, along with her "band of brothers," stormed the British fortifications. As the war dragged on, Sampson's unit continued to engage the enemy, and her ruse remained undetected. It was during her first full-scale battle outside Tarrytown, New York, that she was injured and brought to the hospital field tent, where her true identity was nearly revealed by the doctor that day. After escaping the field hospital, Sampson fled on horseback, stopping only to dig one of the musket balls from her thigh with a knife. She tried desperately to remove the second one, but it was embedded too deeply in her leg and the ball remained there, causing her pain and discomfort for the rest of her life.

Despite her injuries, the thought of fleeing the war never crossed Sampson's mind. She spent several months serving as general's aide while recuperating, then rejoined the continental forces when she was well enough to fight again. Despite the constant throbbing pain in her leg from her Tarrytown injuries, Sampson continued to fight fiercely and honorably. She had several other close calls with death, taking musket balls through her coat and even one through her cap, which seared the hair on the side of her head. While fighting in a later battle, she was hit by another bullet, this time in the shoulder. Though she managed once again to keep her gender a secret during her recuperation, Sampson was soon overcome with fever during an epidemic and slipped into unconsciousness. When she awakened and looked into the eyes of the shocked hospital staff surrounding her bed, she knew the ruse was up.

After receiving an honorable discharge, Sampson returned to Massachusetts. She married Benjamin Gannet of Sharon, Massachusetts, and had three children with him. A book about her remarkable life was written by Herman Mann in 1797, entitled *The Female Review: or, Memoirs of an American Young Lady*. At the encouragement of her old friend Paul Revere, Sampson supplemented her income by embarking on public speaking tours throughout New York and New England. During her performances, she dressed in a male military uniform and performed maneuvers from the manual of arms while sharing her background and wartime experiences with the audience. She petitioned Congress for equal rights, and became the first and only female to secure a full military pension for battlefield service during the Revolutionary War.

Deborah Sampson died of yellow fever in April of 1827. Several statues and monuments were erected honoring her great achievements, and in 1982, the Massachusetts legislature declared May 23—the day she first enlisted in the Continental Army disguised as a man—Deborah Sampson Day.

# TRIEU THI TRINH

*It would be easier to fight a tiger than face Lady Trieu in battle.*

The breathtaking mountains of Vietnam are unique in their luminous beauty. Small pockets of gray rock dot the lush terrain that drops in steep, jagged ridges, to the valleys below.

These mountains were beautiful to most visitors, perhaps, but likely not to the legions of conquering Chinese soldiers who had once again invaded their southern neighbor in the spring of AD 246. Though their previous incursion into Vietnam had gone exceedingly well, they were then dealing with a previously unforeseen—and deadly—complication.

The low rumble was subtle. So subtle at first that they thought it could be an approaching thunderstorm or, perhaps, an earthquake. Though it was neither, the occupying Chinese soldiers who were encamped in that low valley would soon wish it were an earthquake—or anything other than what it really was. As the sound became louder and more ominous, the ground beneath their feet shook violently. And then they saw her.

It was a scene out of a nightmare, something the battle-hardened Chinese forces had never witnessed before—a fearsome female warrior, clad in a blazing yellow robe with war swords clenched in both her fists, charging toward them atop an enormous war elephant. Her bloodcurdling cries filled the air around them, urging her loyal soldiers onward toward the enemy. Unfortunately for the Chinese, this wasn't a bad dream at all. And for many of those Chinese soldiers, the terrifying sight of this Vietnamese woman with the deadly duo of swords bearing down on them would be the last thing they'd ever see.

Often described as the "Vietnamese Joan of Arc," Trieu Thi Trinh's cunning and ruthlessness disrupted China's expansionist plans and wreaked havoc on the invading troops. Though they far outnumbered the defending Vietnamese forces, Trieu Thi Trinh's fearless determination and brutal fighting style repelled the Chinese soldiers' advances not five, not ten, not twenty…but thirty times! Thirty times the Chinese army pushed to take over Trieu Thi Trinh's homeland, and thirty times it was driven back by her forces. Thirty times, the Chinese were forced to retreat, leaving battlefields littered with their slain and wounded soldiers.

Trieu Thi Trinh's imminent showdown with the Chinese was years in the making. Others may have been shocked that a seemingly harmless peasant woman could lead such a deadly and effective insurgency, but Trieu Thi Trinh had long since known her fate. Orphaned as a young girl and raised in a small, poor rural village, Trieu Thi Trinh had witnessed the atrocities of the Chinese forces who regularly invaded her homeland. She swore from a very young age to exact revenge and began preparing for her destiny as the most formidable foe to ever face the enormous Chinese army. She spent time in the mountains, hills, and jungles of her homeland, vigorously training and honing her skills as a warrior. When she emerged, Trieu Thi Thrinh had transformed herself from a young, tough peasant girl into a virtual fighting machine.

When the Eastern Wu Chinese state invaded yet again, the Chinese king expressed his desire for peace. For a few months, it appeared as if Lady Trieu's predictions about everlasting conflict with the Chinese were wrong. Unlike previous Chinese rulers, the Wu king swore to enact respectful measures that would usher in an era of harmonious coexistence between the Vietnamese people and their Chinese occupiers. All he asked in return was that the Vietnamese population relinquish their weapons. Hoping for peace—and facing another possible wholesale slaughter by their longtime enemy— most Vietnamese citizens complied. A jaded and distrustful Lady Trieu, however, did not. Her own brother implored her to follow suit, but she refused to obey the edict. When he repeatedly tried to discourage her from resisting, Lady Trieu finally turned to her brother and, with fire in her eyes, said, "I'd like to ride storms, kill sharks in the open sea, drive out the aggressors, reconquer the country, undo the ties of serfdom, and never bend my back in servitude to a man."

Initially, the Wu king seemed to hold fast to his promise of peaceful cohabitation, but it was all a deceitful ploy. Once most of the population was disarmed, things began to rapidly change. The occupying Chinese became more arrogant, abusive, and disrespectful to the native population. Any Vietnamese citizen who dared object to the treatment was dealt with swiftly and harshly. The time for open rebellion had begun once again, but this time it took the form of a diminutive peasant woman atop an elephant, with rage in her heart, fire in her eyes, and war swords in her fists.

Lady Trieu's next seemingly impossible move was to raise and train an army to drive the Chinese forces from Vietnam. This would be a difficult task even for a seasoned and respected male warrior, but Lady Trieu would bear the extra burden of being a woman in the unlikely position of sparking and leading a military insurgency.

Undeterred, she quickly recruited thousands of Vietnamese citizens, training them in hidden camps throughout the country. Her brother, who had once so desperately tried to persuade her to acquiesce to the Wu king's demands, eagerly joined her army as well. With Lady Trieu as military leader of the Vietnamese guerilla forces, their successes were many and their cause soon caught on with other citizens who became inspired to drive the Chinese back over the border.

The invaders were terrified of Lady Trieu, and rumors soon spread throughout their ranks that this fearsome Vietnamese she-warrior was more than nine feet tall, with glowing red eyes and a battle cry that would drop men to their knees. Though her role as army commander was relatively short, Trieu Thi Trinh's leadership was disastrous for the Chinese. Her elephant charges left many an enemy soldier crushed and maimed in her wake, and the mere sight of her atop the charging beast, with war swords raised high over her head, was terrifying. She knew no fear and always placed herself at the forefront of the attacks.

"It would be easier to fight a tiger than face Lady Trieu in battle!" was a common refrain among the ranks of the Chinese.

Lady Trieu's military successes soon strained the Chinese invaders so much that the emperor dedicated the bulk of his fighting force to defeating her. The sheer size of the Chinese army finally overwhelmed Lady Trieu's much smaller force, and, at great cost to the Chinese, the infamous Vietnamese warrior was finally defeated.

Today, Lady Trieu is a hero in Vietnam. In addition to the many streets and shrines named after her throughout the country, there is also a national holiday honoring her bravery and her contributions to the Vietnamese people.

# Joan of Arc

*I am not afraid. I was born to do this.*

In May of 1429, the siege of Orléans, France, by English armies and their French Burgundian allies had been well under way for more than six months. The English had nearly all of northern France and parts of the southwest, including Paris, under their control. More than a hundred miles away in the royal court at Chinon, a desperate King Charles VII met with his military advisors who were all but convinced that the Anglo-Burgundian forces would soon overrun Orléans. With his beloved France falling deeper into disarray, King Charles began preparations for the eventual surrender, not only of Orléans, but of his entire empire. The tense meeting was abruptly interrupted by a small group of French loyalists who burst into the room. Accompanying this bold group of men was a young peasant girl, who joined them in kneeling before the king.

"Your Highness," one loyalist began, bowing his head as he spoke. "We seek your blessing to travel to Orléans and join our countrymen there."

King Charles looked at the small, ragged group before him in astonishment. "What would be your purpose in doing so?" he asked.

The slight peasant girl, still humbly bowing before him, answered. "By the grace of God, we're going to break the siege, defeat the English, and free France, sire. We just need an army."

King Charles didn't know whether to laugh or have her confined to an asylum for the insane. "Who *are* you?" inquired the king as he stared at her incredulously.

The peasant girl rose slowly to her feet and looked into the king's eyes. "I am Joan of Arc," she said.

It was no idle boast. Impressed with her cool tenacity and unwavering determination, King Charles soon furnished Joan with a small army. On April 27, 1429, she set out for Orléans to defend the realm of France.

It was an incredible undertaking for a woman from such humble beginnings. Joan was born into a poor family in eastern France. The small peasant village of

Domrémy, where she was raised, was an island of French loyalists surrounded by a population more aligned with the pro-English Burgundians. The serene, picturesque countryside where she grew up belied a more tumultuous reality; raids against those loyal to the French crown were common, and, as a young girl, Joan witnessed her own village burned by a Burgundian mob. The influence of the Anglo-Burgundian alliance continued to spread throughout Joan's early years, with skirmishes finally breaking out into full blown war.

Joan claimed to experience supernatural visions, predicting that she herself would lead the campaign to drive the English and their allies from France. The young peasant girl's proposition for the king on that spring day in 1429 must have seemed an outrageous request to all but the extremely confident Joan of Arc and her small band of believers. Perhaps if things had not been so dire for King Charles, his answer may have been different. But King Charles knew his regime was close to collapse and every previous attempt to fend off the English attackers at Orléans had failed. Though it was likely a desperate, last ditch effort on his part to grant the illiterate seventeen-year-old peasant girl's wish to lead his demoralized army, it would prove to be a fortuitous decision.

The king declined to furnish Joan with armor, weapons, or equipment because she was a woman, but these were minor setbacks at best and did nothing to dampen her enthusiasm—or her success. Armor, swords, shields, and horses were either borrowed or donated, and Joan set off to Orléans with her followers, ready for battle.

Though the English siege had lasted over six months, their attack collapsed only nine days after Joan's arrival at the front. She personally led charges in several battles, and on May 7 she was struck by an arrow. She quickly dressed her wound and returned to the fight. On May 8, just as Joan had predicted, the English retreated from Orléans. At a time when the military situation for the French had seemed increasingly bleak, this crucial and decisive victory provided a much-needed turning point in the war. In recognition of her monumental contributions, King Charles granted Joan's request that her hometown of Domrémy be exempt from taxes, an accommodation that provided great financial relief to the poor people of her beloved village.

Joan continued to fight with King Charles' loyalists across France, proving to be invaluable not only on the battlefield, but during military strategy sessions as well. Her previous detractors soon sang her praises, becoming ardent loyalists of the firebrand peasant girl who was leading thousands of hardened French soldiers into battle.

Noblemen and generals alike confirmed that Joan's insight and wisdom strongly impacted their decisions, and the armies she served under enjoyed remarkable success. She was wounded a number of times and suffered a severe blow from a large rock thrown from atop a wall outside the city of Jargeau. Though her helmet saved her life, Joan was knocked unconscious and remained deeply dazed for several hours. Against the field surgeon's orders, she soon returned to the fight and successfully led French forces in the siege and surrender of Jargeau the following day.

It was hard to miss the diminutive peasant girl, even in the heat of battle, as Joan insisted on carrying the large, colorful banner of France into the fray. Her fortitude and uncompromising passion deeply inspired those serving with her, and the once demoralized French forces were rejuvenated in their drive to push the English and their allies from their country.

After a number of successful campaigns, Joan was felled from her horse by an archer while attacking an enemy encampment. She was captured, imprisoned, and charged with heresy, as well as a number of other serious offenses. Ironically, because she wore protective armor in battle—attire worn only by male soldiers at the time—Burgundian officials were able to add the very serious charge of "cross-dressing" to her list of transgressions. She was imprisoned at Beaurevoir Castle, where she was tortured, interrogated several times, and deprived of food, water, and sleep. Despite such brutal conditions, Joan held her own during intense exchanges with church and government authorities. She refused to renounce her faith or her loyalty to France and was sentenced to death. During her imprisonment, Joan made several escape attempts, including one when she jumped from a seventy-foot tower. Though several people involved in the trial all but admitted her persecution was a farce—and the charges against her trumped-up—Joan of Arc was marched to the public square in Rouen, France, on May 30, 1431, and burned at the stake.

Twenty-five years later, in 1456, a posthumous court declared Joan of Arc innocent of all charges. She was beatified as a saint in 1909, and countless plays, movies, books, and songs exist to celebrate her amazing achievements and the powerful mark she left on history.

# TOMOE

*She was a warrior worth a thousand, ready to confront a demon or a god, mounted or on foot.*

The male-dominated samurai warrior culture of Japan—known as the Bushido—was the ruling military class in a country with a long history of conquest and war. Becoming a samurai, though extremely difficult, was an incredible honor. Boys began training at the age of three, when they would learn the basics of fencing and swordsmanship. Though the samurai were required to become masters of all weaponry—including bows, arrows, spears, and guns—the primary weapon and symbol of the elite samurai society was the sword. Being a samurai wasn't an occupation or a career. The Bushido samurai code of honor didn't allow for vacations, personal days, lunch breaks, or overtime. The Bushido code was a way of life. Loyalty to your master was the fundamental focus and the sole reason for living as a samurai warrior. The training was brutal, the competition fierce, and the samurai's commitment to the life of the Bushido was absolute.

While this noble fighting culture consisted predominately of men, the samurai code was defined by honor, loyalty, ability, and intelligence, not sex, and the onna-bugeisha were a small, highly elite warrior class of female samurai. These women received no preferential treatment in either training or battle, and they fought side by side with their male samurai brethren. While all samurai earned their highly respected positions through rigorous and constant training, mental and physical toughness, and fierce loyalty to their masters, one onna-bugeisha in particular stood out among both male and female samurai: Tomoe.

Tomoe's master was a samurai warrior named Yoshinaka of the Minamoto clan. The Minamotos promoted a new vision for Japan that contradicted those who wished to maintain the more established and traditional culture of the country. Among these traditionalists was the Taira clan and its leader, Yoritomo. Tension between these two factions escalated into armed conflict. After the Minamoto clan drove the Taira clan into the countryside, temporarily defeating it, there was a brief respite in the fighting. Hostilities flared again, however, in a military campaign known as the Genpei War—

and this time the outcome would be final, with the victors deciding the fate of Japan.

While Yoshinaka's samurai fought valiantly and bravely for him during the conflict, Tomoe emerged as the most respected and reliable military leader of the war. When not slaying rivals from afar with her deadly archery skills, many a Taira warrior was carried dead or wounded from the field of battle after engaging with Tomoe in one-on-one sword fighting. After witnessing his most loyal onna-bugeisha perform many times in battle, Yoshinaka said of her, "She is a warrior worth a thousand, ready to confront a demon or god, mounted or on foot."

The culmination of the Genpei War occurred during the Battle of Awazu in February of 1184. It was to be a final showdown between the two forces, with the very fate and direction of Japan dependent on the outcome of the battle. Both sides were fiercely committed to their samurai leaders, and every soldier that lined up on the field knew that they were facing an enemy intent on fighting to the death.

The Bushido code dictated that a battle of this magnitude would commence with a duel to the death in the middle of the field between the single best warriors from each side. The tension hung in the air like a thick fog as the Taira's chosen warrior strode to the designated area. With the confidence and bloodlust understood only by the Bushido samurai, he raised his sword menacingly toward the Minamoto clan in a direct challenge. Within moments, the Minamoto army parted and the masked contender from its clan emerged, walking calmly and methodically toward the Taira foe. When the signal was given to begin the duel, the two deadliest samurai warriors in all of Japan raised their swords. The art of samurai sword fighting requires almost super human physical endurance and unimaginable concentration. There is no room for error; even a slight miscalculation usually meant a death sentence. And so it was that day when the Taira warrior made a small but fatal mistake, which resulted in a sword thrust clean through his armor and into his heart. The cheers from the Minamoto side were deafening as their champion struck down the Taira warrior and stood triumphantly over the dying adversary. With moments left to live, the Taira warrior watched in astonishment and shame as the Minamoto warrior removed the samurai war mask and looked into his eyes. Adding insult to deadly injury in the macho samurai culture, the Taira warrior realized he had just been slain by a woman—Tomoe.

Though both of Tomoe's brothers also served under Yoshinaka, Tomoe was selected to lead Yoshinaka's forces into battle. It was a long, bloody day, with both sides suffering heavy losses. In her youth, Tomoe had acquired her superior equestrian skills by riding wild horses through the mountains, a talent that served her well later in battle. At one point, Tomoe was ordered to take out the head samurai of the Taira army, who was leading his troops astride a large horse. Without hesitation, she rode into the midst of the raging battle, flung herself at the warrior, and knocked him from his stallion. She quickly pinned and decapitated him. From there, Tomoe was ordered to single-handedly defend a narrow bridge from approaching enemy forces. Tomoe immediately leapt on a war stallion, killing several enemy soldiers with her sword on her way to secure the bridge. Upon reaching the bridge, she dismounted and engaged the enemy. She fought alone for more than an hour, defending the bridge and slaying several enemy samurai who tried to overcome the lone onna-bugeisha.

The battle eventually turned, but not in Yoshinaka's favor; after he was struck by an arrow and fell, fatally wounded, from his horse, Yoritomo and his Taira army soon gained the upper hand. Not much is known about what happened to Tomoe after the Battle of Awazu, but it is well documented that her grief at seeing her master slain was overwhelming. Some accounts have her joining a nunnery and living a peaceful life of prayer and reflection, but a more likely scenario claims that Tomoe retrieved the severed head of Yoshinaka from the battlefield and walked with it into the sea. She drowned in the angry surf, intending to serve her master for all eternity, a fiercely loyal follower of the samurai warrior code to the end.

# LASKARINA BOUBOULINA

*I will use everything at my disposal to fight for the sake of my nation!*

Most rebel leaders end up in prison. Laskarina Bouboulina was born in one. She could have lived a life of spectacular comfort and luxury. Her trading business was flourishing, her fleet of merchant ships was growing, and her future as a rare female titan of maritime commerce in the 1800s had never looked more promising. But as much as Laskarina enjoyed the excitement, adventure, and challenges in the world of international trade, this extraordinary woman valued something far beyond the respect and prosperity she enjoyed as a wildly successful shipping tycoon—freedom for her beloved country of Greece.

Given Laskarina's lineage, her success in both business and in war was unsurprising. Her father, Stavrianos Pinotsis, a successful sea captain from the Greek island of Hydra, had been active in the struggle for Greek independence against the Turkish Ottomans. After participating in a failed rebellion, Stavrianos Pinotsis was imprisoned in Constantinople, where Laskarina was later born while her mother was visiting him. It was a fortuitous event, with Laskarina barely avoiding the same fate years later as she, like her father before her, also fought against the Ottomans. Had they known just how much trouble Pinotsis's daughter would cause them in the future, they likely would have locked her up alongside her rebellious father the day she was born.

Stavrianos Pinotsis died in captivity and Laskarina's mother eventually remarried, settling on the island of Spetses. It was while living on Spetses that Laskarina developed a deep love for the ocean, adventure, and shipping. She sat mesmerized as sailors, merchants, and Greek patriots shared tales of their travels, travesties, and successes while conducting business around the world. An enduring bond with the people of Spetses flourished within her, along with a shared and bitter hatred for the Turkish Ottoman Empire. The Turks had dominated and decimated their island for more than 400 years, and even at that young age, Laskarina vowed to continue the fight against Ottoman oppression with whatever resources were available to her. Years later, she would find herself in a position with far more power and resources than she ever could have imagined.

By 1811, Laskarina had been married and widowed twice. Her second husband, Dimitrios Bouboulis, left her with seven children and a substantial shipping empire. Unlike most women of the time—who might have known precious little about their husbands' ventures—Laskarina was well positioned to assume control of the business. She not only maintained the vast operations, but rapidly expanded them. She increased the lines of imports and exports, developed an expansive network of global partnerships, and built four more ships to add to an already immense business empire.

Laskarina became even more successful and well-known in the maritime trading world than her husband, and her activities did not go unnoticed by the watchful eye of the Ottomans. The Turks still controlled most of the shipping lanes and merchant business where Laskarina conducted her most lucrative ventures, and it wasn't long before they made a move to confiscate her holdings. Claiming that her deceased husband, Dimitrios Bouboulis, had aided the Russians during the Russo-Turkish War, the Ottomans attempted to utilize military force to bring Laskarina and her enterprises under their control. The cunning Greek patriot was one step ahead of them, however, and she quickly embarked on a diplomatic expedition to Constantinople, seeking help from the Russian ambassador stationed there. She successfully enlisted the help of the Russians, who ensured her protection from the Ottomans. Though Laskarina had temporarily thwarted her longtime enemy, the Ottomans made it clear they wouldn't be held at bay for long. They had taken off the gloves and were looking for a fight, and Laskarina was only too happy to oblige. She had waited a long time to avenge the people who had murdered and oppressed her fellow Greeks, imprisoned her father, and razed her beloved island of Spetses.

The seeds of independence, though suppressed for a time, started to sprout again in the hearts and minds of the Greek people. Laskirina joined an underground movement called Filiki Etaireia, an organization formed to fight the Turks once again and finally establish a free Greek state. Due to her resources, loyalty, and commitment to the cause of independence, she was the only woman allowed to be a part of Filiki Etaireia. At great risk to herself, her children, and her fortune, Laskirina began funding the group's operations. Utilizing her vast network of contacts developed from years in global trade, she began smuggling large shipments of arms, ammunition, food, and supplies to the rebels. Her fleet of ships proved invaluable, first in smuggling operations and later in active combat. The flagship of her fleet was the *Agamemnon*, a large warship she had constructed while bribing the Turkish officials to look the other way. The ship then sailed safely to Spetses, where it was outfitted for battle. The timing of the *Agamemnon's* arrival bode well for the Greek patriots, for just days later, the war of independence exploded on Spetses.

The ship was armed with eighteen heavy cannon and the flag of Greek independence flew proudly from its main sail. Of the eight vessels that sailed off to enforce a naval blockade at two of the Ottoman controlled ports, five belonged to Laskirina. The fighting was fierce—on both land and sea—and, despite losing her son during the conflict, Laskirina, at the helm of the *Agamemnon*, and her fellow patriots surged forward. She took part in the conquest and capture of two Ottoman controlled port towns thought to be invulnerable, and she rescued a number of women being held in forced servitude to a Turkish sultan. Though she depleted her fortune, lost a number of family members, and sacrificed virtually all she had in the war of independence, Laskarina lived to see her dream of a Greek state free from Ottoman rule.

After surviving a life replete with danger in both war and in commerce on the high seas, Laskarina was ironically shot to death in her own home during a family dispute in 1825.

In honor of her immense contributions to Greek independence and for fighting so selflessly for the Soviets, Laskarina Bouboulina was posthumously awarded the title of first female admiral of the Russian navy.

# Lyudmila Pavlichenko

*I wear my uniform with honor. It has been covered with blood in battle.*

The advancing German soldier was dead before the sound of the rifle ever reached his ears. The other members of his platoon quickly dropped to the ground, hugging the cold, barren Russian soil outside of Sevastopol.

"Where did the bullet come from?" the squad leader shouted.

A soldier raised his head slightly, carefully scanning the horizon in front of them.

"I think it—" He never finished his sentence as another bullet pierced his helmet, killing him instantly. The entire squad of German soldiers was pinned down under the deadly accurate fire of a lone Russian sniper. And they knew just who she was.

When German troops poured onto Soviet soil in June of 1942, Lyudmila Pavlichenko rushed to join the Soviet army and defend her homeland. Due to her gender, she was initially denied entry into any of the armed units that were mobilizing to confront the enemy advance. Soviet army officials persuaded her to take up nursing duties, a contribution they felt was more appropriate for a woman. Being eager to help, Lyudmila reluctantly joined the nurse corps, but her superiors learned soon enough that her interests and skills lay elsewhere. While accompanying a small group of Russian soldiers on a mission, Lyudmila and her comrades found themselves trapped on a hill surrounded by the enemy. The Russians were suffering heavy casualties, and when it appeared as though the Germans were close to overtaking their position, one of Lyudmila's superiors handed her a rifle and desperately ordered her to return fire. He watched in amazement as she quickly dispatched two enemy soldiers, halting their attack with her deadly accurate fire and inspiring her compatriots to counterattack with renewed vigor. Lyudmila Pavilchenko's reputation as the deadliest female sniper in history was born.

Her interest in shooting and marksmanship had begun with a simple childhood challenge. "When a neighbor's boy boasted of his exploits at a shooting range, I set out to show that a girl could do just as well," she recalled during a later interview. "So I practiced a lot. After our first contest, he never challenged me again."

With her interest now piqued, Lyudmila developed a strong interest in firearms and was eager to display her expertise long before she was handed a rifle that day on the hill. She spent much of her spare time working on her new hobby and eventually joined a shooting club. When not working at her factory job, Lyudmila trained relentlessly, learning all she could about firearms and perfecting her sharpshooting skills. Her training paid off, and she quickly earned recognition as a notable and respected amateur sharpshooter. She could never have guessed how valuable those hours on the range would become later on in life.

Before the war, she married young and gave birth to a son, but divorced her husband soon after. While Lyudmila was attending Kiev University in the Ukraine and working toward a master's degree in history, the German army commenced its attack on the Soviet Union.

Though nearly two thousand female snipers would eventually fight for the Red Army during World War II, Lyudmila Pavlichenko was best known to the German soldiers she faced on the battlefield, and one of only about five hundred Russian female snipers who survived the war. Her success as a sniper is astonishing. Lyudmila made 187 of her total 209 confirmed kills within her first seventy-five days as a sniper, averaging an astounding 2.5 kill shots per day. She was wounded several times, but only removed from battle once after she was struck in the face with shrapnel. By the time she was promoted to sergeant, she had 257 confirmed kills and was extolled by the Southern Army War Council for her service. Her response?

"I'll get more."

There are many skills that are required to be an expert sniper, and shooting proficiency is only one such component. A single mistimed movement or a poor choice of hiding place can result in instant death. Patience, instinct, speed and accuracy, along with nerves of steel and an iron will all have to align and culminate in a split-second action. Lyudmila Pavlichenko had all these talents and more. In addition to having a deeply ingrained killer instinct, she could lay still undetected for hours. Her high kill count was all the more remarkable given that her weapon of choice was the Soviet bolt-action Struger, an almost obsolete rifle at the time.

While the Germans would have preferred to take her out on the battlefield, they were so desperate to remove Lyudmila from the war that they regularly tried to convert her to their side. Using both propaganda pamphlets and radio broadcasts, they offered her everything from an officership in the German army to chocolates.

Lyudmila, of course, refused, which resulted in the Germans threatening to tear her into 309 pieces—one for each of the German soldiers she had killed up to that point.

"At least they know my score," Lyudmila quipped upon hearing of the threat. "I look forward to them tearing me into twice that amount!"

While her 309 documented kills places her within the top five snipers of all time, her actual number is likely much higher. In order to fall into the "confirmed" category, a kill had to be witnessed by a third party and Lyudmila spent most of her fighting time in the field alone. She not only killed hundreds of rank and file German troops, but almost single-handedly decimated the Nazis' top brass, as well as their elite and invaluable sniper force. Among the many recipients of her deadly craft were more than one hundred German officers and thirty-six of the top snipers in the German army. Increasingly desperate, the Germans placed a bounty on Lyudmila's head. Far from being intimidated, Lyudmila pressed her superiors for more time in the field. During one battle, after Lyudmila had killed several soldiers, the Germans were finally able to locate her general position. They directed a barrage of mortar fire, peppering the area with explosions. Lyudmila Pavlichenko was struck by shrapnel and carried off the field of battle by her comrades.

After recovering from her wounds, the Soviet command decided Lyudmila could best contribute to the war effort by training the next wave of young snipers eager to fight the Nazis. Though devastated that she had been taken off the front lines, Lyudmila set to work teaching the eager new recruits the secrets of her lethal craft. She was even sent to the United States to garner support for the war effort, becoming the first Soviet citizen to be received at the White House.

After the war, Pavlichenko went back to finish her master's degree at Kiev University. Upon completing her education, she became the historian she had always

hoped to be, and was also active in the Soviet Committee of the Veterans of War. Included among her many accolades are books, songs, a film, and at least two commemorative stamps bearing her likeness. Lyudmila Pavlichenko died October 10, 1974, at age fifty-eight, and is buried in the famed Novodevichy Cemetery in Moscow.

# LOZEN

*She could ride, shoot, and fight like a man.*

It was spring, 1878, just outside the San Carlos Apache Indian Reservation in Arizona. The lieutenant held up his hand and pulled on the reins of his horse. The column of U.S. Cavalry soldiers under his command came to a slow halt behind him. On the horizon before them was a lone Native American, also on horseback, slowly approaching. The lieutenant squinted at the figure as he reached for his army-issue binoculars. He could almost feel the tension of his soldiers as they, too, stared nervously at the approaching figure. A sergeant galloped up from the rear and made his way to the lieutenant's side. "Apache?" he asked.

Still staring through his binoculars, the lieutenant nodded. "Apache, for sure. And it's a woman." He turned in his saddle to face his men. "At ease!" he commanded, his body starting to relax. "It's just a lone squaw."

While the reassuring words of the lieutenant put the rest of the column at ease, the wiser and more war-weary sergeant took no such comfort. When he peered through his own binoculars at the solitary figure approaching them, he recognized her right away. And his blood froze.

"Lieutenant…" the sergeant said, his voice cracking with fear. The lieutenant turned in time to see the Apache woman racing toward them, war club held ominously over her head, as the prairie around them sprang to life with Apache warriors who had been hiding in the scrub. Arrows, gunshots, and the war cries of the Apache filled the air.

"God help us," the sergeant whispered to himself as he eyed the ferocious woman bearing down on them. "It's Lozen…"

By 1872, the Apache chief Victorio had already conceded defeat and led his tribe—including his sister Lozen—onto the dreaded San Carlos Reservation in Arizona. The conditions on the reservations were so deplorable, it was known as "Hell's Forty Acres." The Apache were, by nature, a nomadic people, and Victorio had not gone willingly. Although the white man had made promises of peace and had assured him that the Apache people would be treated fairly, Victorio was justifiably suspicious. Almost immediately, the U.S. Army demonstrated great animosity and disdain for the Native Americans living in the San Carlos Reservation. The promised food, housing, and medical care never materialized, and soldiers, as well as their commanding officers, began brutally torturing and killing the Apache people. To add insult to injury, the white man then started seizing land that was supposed to be the property of the reservation. The government's forced relocation of the tribe to the reservation subjected them to a life that, in many ways, was akin to slavery. By 1877, the Apache had lost patience with the white man's promises, and the chief and a band of loyalists decided to once again fight back. As they readied their weapons and prepared their horses, Victorio watched proudly as Lozen swiftly mounted her palomino. She glanced over at her brother, returning his smile.

"Save some soldiers for me," he said. Lozen grabbed the reins of her horse with her left hand and raised her rifle into the air.

"Like the white man, I make no true promises," she replied before riding off.

Even as a young girl, Lozen had scant interest in the tribe's traditional female occupations; while other Apache girls gravitated toward domestic affairs, Lozen followed in her brother's footsteps, eager to train in the ways of the warrior. She was eager, too, to learn the art of healing, and became a greatly revered Apache medicine woman. She was also a brilliant military strategist, a fierce fighter, and a master of ambushes and surprise attacks. Her fearless battlefield tactics wreaked havoc on the U.S. soldiers, and she quickly became a respected and feared fighter.

"Lozen is my right hand...strong as a man, braver than most, and cunning in strategy. Lozen is a shield to her people," Victorio proclaimed.

Unfortunately, she could not be his shield when he most needed it; Chief Victorio died in battle while Lozen was accompanying an Apache mother and her newborn baby back to the reservation. When word reached Lozen of her brother's death, she rode to the battle site to aid the survivors and engage any enemy soldiers unfortunate enough to cross her path. While grieving the loss of her cherished brother, Lozen nourished a burning commitment to exact revenge on her people's oppressors. With the Apache in disarray and on the run, other native factions fought U.S. troops, and she sought to join them. After successfully eluding several attempts to capture her, Lozen joined Chief Geronimo's warriors, who were waging their own fight against her sworn enemy. She fought bravely alongside the famed Apache chief, and legend has it she could sense the enemy's location, track its movement, and accurately determine the number of troops simply by reaching out her arms toward the sky. After Geronimo's eventual defeat and surrender to United States authorities, Lozen herself was finally captured. She was held in such high esteem by both her native people and her enemies that she was allowed to participate in negotiations that would determine the fate of the Apache people.

While she successfully petitioned for an agreement that spared the lives of Geronimo and his supporters, and also guaranteed their freedom, Lozen died of tuberculosis as a prisoner of war. Her body was returned to her tribe so it could be buried in a place of honor according to Apache tradition. Lozen's legend still lives on in Apache society today, where she is honored and celebrated through storytelling and dance.

# BOUDICCA

*This is a woman's resolve; as for men, they may live and be slaves.*

It didn't have to be this way.

Though his wounds were not mortal, the Roman general knew he was about to die. He lay on his back in the blood-soaked dirt and stared up at the Celtic warrior who hovered over him. He recognized the face, the flowing red hair, the piercing blue eyes of his executioner. Not long ago, he had assaulted and tortured her and her two daughters. Yes, he had witnessed a number of expressions on this woman's face, but he'd never seen her smile. Until then. Fortunately for him, it was a relatively quick death. There was still a battle raging around them, there were more Roman soldiers to slay, and Boudicca, the female warrior about to kill him, had much to do.

"I am Boudicca," she said. "This is not for me, but for my daughters, for my people, for justice!" And with that, she gave the sword a final thrust, pinning his now lifeless body to the ground.

Boudicca was a queen, wife of Prasutagus, the Celtic king of the Iceni tribe, who was initially an ally of the Romans. Prasutagus had drawn up a will stipulating that upon his death, his kingdom would be divided equally with one half going to Nero, emperor of Rome, and the other half shared by his two daughters. However, when Prasutagus passed away, Nero broke the agreement—claiming that only sons could inherit property—and ordered his army to invade Prasutagus's kingdom. To add to the humiliation, Boudicca and her daughters were whipped, tortured, and raped. The Roman general in charge of the assaults thought this would terrorize Boudicca into submission and enable him to gain control of her kingdom.

It was a fatal miscalculation.

The emperor's betrayal and his cruel treatment of Boudicca, her daughters, and their people by the invading Roman soldiers enraged the fiery Celtic queen. She not only pledged to drive the Romans from their land, but she intended to slaughter as many of them as possible along the way. In addition to her own Iceni people, Boudicca rallied and unified other local tribes to join the insurrection and seek revenge on the

Romans. The speed with which she was able to assemble and train her army took Roman officials completely by surprise. She commanded more than 100,000 warriors.

Standing in her war chariot and flanked by her daughters, Boudicca addressed her followers, "It is not as a woman descended from noble ancestry, but as one of the people that I am avenging lost freedom, my scourged body, the outraged chastity of my daughters…This is a woman's resolve; as for men, they may live and be slaves!"

Boudicca and her rebel army cut a bloody swath through what is the modern day United Kingdom. The first city to fall under her sword was Camulodunum (now Colchester), which was the Roman capital of Britain at the time, followed by Londinium (London), and finally Verulamium (St. Albans). Driven by personal vengeance as well as loyalty to her tribe, Boudicca and her warriors proved a worthy and vicious foe, often exceeding even the notoriously bloodthirsty Roman army in their cruelty and mercilessness. The rebel army slaughtered, burned, and decimated everything in its path, killing upwards of 80,000 people.

Boudicca rode into battle in a war chariot, her chest plate gleaming in the sun. She held the reins in one hand and slayed enemy soldiers with the spear she wielded in the other. Her successes were so swift, so successful, and so bloody, that Nero was nearly forced to abandon Britain altogether. While her fierce determination and drive undoubtedly contributed to her victorious military conquests, it is also likely that those very same characteristics led to her eventual defeat. A hot temper and inflexible stubbornness can be both friend and foe, and neither helped Boudicca in her final showdown with her most despised nemesis.

Boudicca's forces faced a large, well-trained Roman army in a flat, open field. Her final fight was a debacle, and her rebel army was decimated. Boudicca slew many soldiers and survived the battle, but at the prospect of being taken prisoner, it is said that the proud Celtic queen drank poison and died on the battlefield next to the fallen bodies of her fellow warriors. What became of her daughters is unknown.

Boudicca to this day is still a much admired figure in the United Kingdom, with many finding inspiration from her fighting spirit, stubborn resolve, and willingness to give all for family and nation. A large, beautifully imposing bronze sculpture of the Celtic warrior queen is on display in London, showing her astride her war chariot and flanked by her beloved daughters.

# QUEEN NANNY

*Loved by all, but her enemies. An outstanding military leader who became a symbol of strength for her people.*

It was going to be a very bad day on the plantation—and, this time, not for the slaves. Wielding machetes, muskets, pistols, clubs, and swords, the attacking force of Windward Maroon fighters, led by the fierce and fearless Queen Nanny, descended on the beautiful and expansive grounds of the Jamaican sugar plantation. They quickly overran the grounds of the estate, slaying the British overlords and yielding an impressive cache of much-needed food, weapons, clothing, and other supplies. In addition to the ample bounty secured by the attack, Queen Nanny and her soldiers also freed the many slaves who had been forced into brutal servitude working the sugar cane fields. They then fled back to the safety of their rebel colony, hidden deep in the mountains of Jamaica. It was not the first successful raid by Queen Nanny and her followers, and local authorities knew it would not be the last.

Queen Nanny was born around 1686, into a large family on the west coast of Africa. Though she descended from African royalty, an intertribal conflict resulted in Queen Nanny and several of her relatives being captured and sold into slavery. They ended up in Jamaica, where they were sold yet again and forced to work on one of the many plantations scattered throughout the islands. The primary crop was sugarcane, and slaves toiled under extremely harsh conditions in order to cultivate, harvest, and process the lucrative commodity. During her time as a slave, Queen Nanny and her family became acquainted with the Maroons, a defiant Jamaican sect who fled their oppressive existence as slaves on the plantations and formed their own rebel communities in the rugged, hilly interior of the island. Though they were brave, skilled fighters, anxious to free their island of the tyrants who had taken the Jamaican people hostage, the Maroons were disorganized and divided. They lacked a leader who could unify, inspire, and guide them to victory over the English.

They would soon find just such a figure in an impassioned runaway female slave from a land far from their own.

Female slaves on the sugar cane plantations fared no better than the men; marriage was forbidden among the slave population and children were often separated from their mothers and fathers, and then sold. Her brutal experience in bondage did nothing to quell Queen Nanny's defiant spirit, and it wasn't long before she and her brothers escaped into the Jamaican countryside to join the Windward Maroons, one of the two bands fighting the English oppressors.

In short order, Queen Nanny proved to be more than just another loyal soldier in the fight for freedom. She soon became the military leader of the Windward Maroons, developing a reputation among her British foes as a ferocious warrior. She became a master of guerilla warfare and trained the Windward Maroons in the art of camouflage, instructing her soldiers how to "disappear" into the tropical terrain by covering themselves in branches and leaves. There was no shortage of hiding places and useful ambush spots in the mountainous terrain that surrounded the plantations in the valleys below. The lowland rain forests and jungles proved extremely challenging– and deadly–for British troops, who were more accustomed to fighting in open, flat fields. Like fish out of water, the king's soldiers soon found their swords, uniforms, and long muskets snagged by the vines and thick undergrowth of the jungle. Queen Nanny trained her soldiers to use the mountainous battlegrounds to their advantage. The British troops fruitlessly pursued them as booby traps and ambushes wreaked havoc on their numbers and left the survivors physically, mentally, and emotionally drained. Even the most hardy and seasoned veterans of the British crown felt their nerves fray each time they ventured into the unfamiliar and hostile Jamaican terrain.

In addition to her ongoing successful military campaigns against the better equipped British forces, Queen Nanny was notorious for raiding plantations, freeing slaves, and terrorizing anyone associated with the colonizing invaders. As British losses mounted, Queen Nanny's notoriety and fame spread. The size of her guerilla army swelled as countless freed slaves rushed to join the insurgency. Finally, the British colonial government relented and called for negotiations. British attempts to strong-arm Nanny at the negotiating table and force her into unfavorable terms fell flat.

"You are more desperate for peace than I," she shot back. She had them backed into a corner and they knew it.

Reluctantly, British authorities agreed to cease hostilities and honor the terms set forth by Queen Nanny. The treaty stipulated that she and her Maroon followers would no longer be sought by British forces, and that Jamaican land would be allocated where the Maroons and their ancestors could forever live in freedom and peace. The land became known as Nanny Town, a self-sustaining community where the Maroons raised animals, grew crops, and thrived. Always vigilant—and forever distrusting of the notoriously deceitful British occupiers—Queen Nanny ensured the settlement overlooked a ridge that provided the Maroons with a superior advantage in case of attack. The British wisely honored the agreement, knowing that if they failed to do so, the wrath of the indomitable warrior queen would bear down upon them from the imposing mountains like a typhoon. A woman that they had once forced into servitude had the upper hand—a hand they knew all too well could quickly turn into a fist.

In addition to her prowess as a military commander, Queen Nanny is credited with uniting the Maroon factions across Jamaica and played a major role in the preservation of African culture and knowledge. During a period of thirty years, she freed more than 1,000 slaves, subjugated the island's slave trading British overlords, and established a colony of free Jamaicans. She is celebrated today as a historical figure of great reverence and inspiration.

# Maryiya Oktyabrskaya

*My only wish is to kill the Nazi dogs who killed my husband.*

The request was so bizarre that Stalin initially thought it had to be some sort of strange prank.

"Are you sure this isn't a joke?" he asked the aide who stood nervously before him with the letter in his hand.

"We thought that, too, originally," the aide replied. "But our intelligence confirms that this woman does exist, that her husband was killed fighting the enemies of the Motherland, and the money—all 50,000 rubles—is, indeed, in the National Bank. She is just awaiting your reply, comrade."

Stalin was intrigued but still baffled by the contents of the letter and what the widowed woman who wrote it was asking of him. "So let me understand you properly. This woman has sent 50,000 rubles so that we can buy a tank for our forces?"

"Yes, but she not only wants to buy the tank, she also wants to be trained in its use, and she insists upon being taken to the front lines," the aide added.

While it was not uncommon for citizens to donate time, money, and materials toward the war effort, this was the first occasion in which a private citizen–and a woman, no less–not only wanted to purchase a weapon of such magnitude, but also insisted on being the one to personally operate it.

"Why would she want to do such a thing?" Stalin asked, bewildered.

"She writes, 'to kill the Nazi dogs who killed my husband,'" the aide replied, reading from the letter in his hand.

Maria Oktyabrskaya, the mysterious widow from the Ukraine who penned the letter, was not making an idle boast. When she learned that her husband had been killed fighting German forces, her grief turned to rage. She sold all that she owned, deposited her life savings of 50,000 rubles—no small sum in 1941—and penned her proposition to Stalin. And then she waited.

While it took nearly two years for her letter to reach the Russian leader, it was worth the wait. His response was swift and his reply short. "Yes."

Maria Oktyabrskaya was raised a simple peasant girl, one of ten children from a poor Ukrainian family. After marrying a Soviet military officer in 1925, she developed a deep interest in military matters. In addition to nursing skills, she learned how to use weapons, operate vehicles, and fix and repair machinery. Despite her steely determination and her experience with machinery, Maria wasn't taken very seriously at first by instructors at the tank school where she would be trained to operate the T-34 medium Soviet tank she had purchased. After she christened her tank *Fighting Girlfriend*—even painting the name on the turret—there were many in her unit who were convinced that her efforts were nothing more than an elaborate publicity stunt. Their opinions would quickly change, however, when Maria's unit was sent to the front.

Her first battle took place on 21 October, 1943, against the German forces and her deadly skills on the battlefield were soon revealed. Maria and her tank crew took out several artillery guns and machine gun nests, killing more than thirty men. After *Fighting Girlfriend* was disabled by a mortar round, Maria sprang from her tank under heavy fire, toolbox in hand. Enemy bullets ricocheted around her as she repaired the tank, stopping only to fire off a couple of rounds from her sidearm. She then calmly crawled back inside her tank again and continued wreaking havoc on the German forces.

A Soviet commander observing her battlefield exploits said aloud, "She's better than most men."

"Better than most *groups* of men," his comrade replied, correcting him.

After her first battle, Maria's reputation as a reliable, fearless, and effective warrior was solidified and she was immediately promoted to sergeant. Her bravery and fighting expertise in her next battle confirmed that that her success wasn't just a case of beginner's luck. Next, the crew of *Fighting Girlfriend* engaged in a night attack on the town of Novoye Selo, once again proving their mettle under intense combat conditions. After scoring direct hits on a number of German positions, *Fighting Girlfriend* was struck by a German shell, knocking the tank track out and bringing Maria and her crew to a grinding halt. As in the previous battle, Maria jumped from the tank with her tools and set to work fixing *Fighting Girlfriend* as the battle raged around her. Her loyal crew provided covering fire as Maria worked away, seemingly oblivious to the bullets, shells, and explosions all around her. She again repaired the tank, took over command of *Fighting Girlfriend*, and rejoined the battle, directing deadly fire into the ranks of the Nazi troops.

Her Soviet comrades weren't the only ones to take note of Maria Oktyabrskaya's deadly expertise; the German army was well aware of *Fighting Girlfriend* and its infamous commander. They dubbed Maria "Black Death," and a lucrative bounty was soon placed on her head. After months of skirmishes where Maria and her crew continued their deadly assaults against the invading Germans, her luck ran out.

Another nighttime assault on January 17, 1944, would prove to be her last. Maria guided *Fighting Girlfriend* into the deepest part of the fighting, plowing over German defenses and destroying machine gun nests along the way. The crew killed several enemy soldiers and were advancing on another hostile position when a German anti-artillery shell immobilized the tank. For the third time, Maria climbed out of the tank and exposed herself to gunfire as she set to task repairing her beloved *Fighting Girlfriend*. Her crack mechanic skills enabled her to once again repair the tank, but this time, as she climbed toward the turret to get back inside, an explosion knocked her to the ground. She was rushed from the battlefield to a Russian military hospital, metal shrapnel from the shell lodged deep in her brain. Maria spent two months in a coma, fighting as hard for her life as she did on the battlefield, but on March 15, 1944, she succumbed to her wounds and passed away.

Though her fighting career was brief, her impact commanding *Fighting Girlfriend* was legendary. Maria was posthumously awarded the Gold Star medal of the Hero of the Soviet Union, the highest commendation in Russia, and she was laid to rest having avenged the death of her beloved husband many times over.

# JANEQUEO

*She was more dangerous when you couldn't see her.*

It wasn't a cloud, but arrows that blotted out the steaming midday sun. The Spanish conquistadors attacking the fort of the native Chileans were forced once again to scramble for their lives as the deadly deluge rained down upon them. They had been attacking the fort for days, suffering heavy losses in their futile attempt to defeat the Mapuche tribe. A lone warrior appeared on the walls of the fort, spear held high overhead. Though the distance was great, the Spanish commander knew the brave warrior was staring into his eyes. He could feel it. The warrior smiled, beckoning with the spear and urging the Spaniard to come closer in a pretense of welcome. The conquistador commander was being humiliated in front of his own troops and he was furious. Shaking with rage, he rose to his feet, emerging from the safety of the rock where he had been hiding.

"I will have your head before the day is over!" he screamed.

The warrior on the rampart laughed, further enraging the Spanish leader. He signaled to his men to prepare for another attack against the native forces, but soon found himself stumbling for cover behind the rock once more as arrows rained down around them. The screams of his soldiers filled the air as the arrows again found their marks, and, for the first time in his military career, the commander ordered his men to retreat.

The commander and his men fled into the jungle, stumbling over the dense underbrush and vines that hampered their escape. Turning, he caught a final glimpse of the Indian leader who was now dancing and howling on the walls in celebration of their victory.

"Curse her," the Spanish commander seethed. "Curse that woman!"

Tragically for him, it wouldn't be his last encounter with Janequeo, the legendary Mapuche heroine and leader of the only Chilean tribe to have, at that point, defeated the Spanish army. And defeat was not something the Spanish conquerors were accustomed to. It was the 1500s, and Spain was drunk with the arrogance and entitlement that came with being a world superpower. Seeking gold, silver, diamonds, wood, and a host of other plentiful natural resources, hordes of Spanish explorers, adventure-seekers, merchants, mercenaries, and soldiers poured into the native territories of South America like an insatiable horde. They pillaged the land and the Indian people alike as their expansion moved across the continent. After initially being tricked and traumatized into submission, the Mapuche and other native people began to fight back.

Janequeo's disdain for the Spanish conquistadors ran deeper than even the most vengeful victims of the European invasion. Her desire to wipe them out, in fact, was deeply personal; her husband, Huepotaen, the brave and beloved chief of their tribe, and had been captured, tortured, and executed by the Spanish.

She vowed revenge and, indeed, it was revenge she would have.

Fort Puchanqui was the newest and most formidable garrison of those in the Spanish possession. The conquistadors had advanced weaponry, seasoned troops, and a commander dedicated to fulfilling his mission of subduing the rebellious tribe and its leader.

In the end, none of it mattered.

After years of brutal oppression, the Mapuche had had ample time to observe the ways of their Spanish enemies and adopted many of the very same military tactics that had been used against them. The Mapuche mastered horseback riding, eventually developing their own cavalry. In addition to bows, arrows, clubs, and spears, they became proficient in the use of captured cannon and firearms, wreaking havoc on the Spanish with their own weapons. They employed camouflage techniques and booby traps that decimated the Spaniards and showed little or no mercy to any enemy unfortunate enough to be captured. The lush green foliage of the Brazilian jungle soon ran red with rivers of Spanish blood. The tide had turned since Spain's initial incursion onto the Mapuche lands, and the invaders found themselves forced into defensive positions. The natives were tougher, smarter, and far more resilient than the Spaniards had ever imagined. And having a bold, brutal commander like Janequeo leading the native forces made matters progressively worse for the once domineering conquerors.

Under Janequeo's direction, the Mapuche soldiers initiated a military strategy that greatly confused and demoralized the Spanish forces. Natives attacked day or night, usually without warning, then quickly disappeared like ghosts into the thick Chilean jungle. There were no defined battle lines, no boundaries, and no formal rules of engagement. An encounter with the Mapuche could have involved Spanish and native forces facing off in a traditional battle setting, or an attack might have consisted of a lone, lethal, silent arrow streaking from out of a quiet jungle and piercing the throat of a random Spanish conquistador eating dinner with his comrades.

When the attack commenced that day on Fort Puchanqui, the Spanish commander, though confident, knew the stakes were too high to leave anything to chance. The Mapuche adversaries gathered en masse to attack the Spanish stronghold, and the conquistadors scrambled about in last-minute preparations. The native forces had much to fight for, and the Spaniards were on edge, knowing they would likely have to fight to the death. The only thing the Spanish commander sought that day, more than the subjugation of the rebellious native people, was to personally slaughter Janequeo, his hated nemesis and the indomitable female warrior he couldn't seem to defeat. The faith in his men, in his weapons, and in the false security offered by the walls of Fort Puchanqui proved to be in vain as the Mapuche warriors soon breeched the fortifications and swarmed into the Spanish stronghold. Despite the enemy incursion and the precarious situation in which his troops now found themselves, the Spanish commander's sole intent was to confront and slay the native leader who had humiliated him so many times before. As the battle raged around him, he spotted her.

Sword drawn, he crept slowly toward her, watching as she laid waste to several of his soldiers with her war club. Undeterred by the battle raging around him, he crept closer, like a predator stalking his prey, until he was within earshot of the Mapuche commander. His rage boiling over, he screamed over the din of the battle. "Janequeo!"

Hearing his voice, Janequeo turned and faced him.

"Today, this *man* sends that *woman* to hell!" he said, stepping forward with his sword pointed ominously toward her.

Janequeo's calm response was simply, "Today, this *commander* sends that commander to hell first."

When she smiled and stepped forward to meet him, the Spanish leader's blood froze.

The fight didn't last long, and by the time Janequeo rode slowly out of the fort with the Spanish commander's head on the end of her spear, most of the his forces lay dead or dying inside their seemingly impenetrable fort.

The battle was a great victory for Janequeo and the Mapuche people, and they continued to fight the Spanish invaders for years after. While Janequeo and her warriors enjoyed many victories against the conquistadors and their allies, time dragged on and the Spanish presence and military might grew to overwhelming proportions.

Janequeo and her warriors were eventually forced to seek permanent refuge deep in the Chilean countryside. They were never captured by the Spanish and continued to haunt the dreams of the invaders for years after they had disappeared forever into the haunting, impenetrable jungle.

# Ching Shih

*That which is worth living for, is worth dying for!*

The Chinese generals stood nervously before the emperor as he studied the military map spread out on the table. The generals had been tasked with stopping a notoriously successful pirate that had terrorized the shipping lanes and coastal villages of China and Southeast Asia for almost a decade. They didn't have good news.

"The Portuguese navy?" the emperor inquired. You could hear a pin drop in the room. The generals seemed to freeze in place, too petrified to answer. After a pause that seemed to last an eternity, one finally felt compelled to address the emperor's question.

"Decimated, Your Imperial Highness."

A second uncomfortable pause filled the room as the emperor redirected his attention to the map. He pointed to the China Strait, where most of the pirate attacks had been occurring. "The British navy is unbeatable," he began confidently. "They assured me they have ample resources to confront the pirates."

"Your Imperial Highness," a second general murmured apologetically. "The British have been defeated. What remains of their fleet is now sailing back to England."

The emperor's icy stare softened into a look of saddened acceptance and defeat. After another eternal silence, one particularly brave general bowed and posed the question they'd all been dreading to ask. "What should we do now?"

The emperor looked up at the group of terrified, utterly defeated military men and said the words he'd been avoiding for more than a decade. "Negotiate with her."

While no doubt humiliating for the leader of such a powerful nation, the Chinese emperor had little choice. Ching Shih wasn't just a pirate; she was the commander of the largest pirate fleet in history, and the most successful buccaneer the world would ever know.

Ching Shih was an unusually attractive girl and had been forced into prostitution at a young age. While working on a floating brothel in Canton Harbor, she had a visit one night from a notorious celebrity of the time, a dashing pirate named Zhèng Yi. He was

47

the famous commander of a fleet of pirate ships known as the Red Flag Fleet. Zhèng Yi's intention that night was to visit the brothel for some salacious entertainment, not fall in love. But as soon as he laid his eyes on the stunning Ching Shih, fall in love he did.

Her intellect and business acumen were even more impressive than her beauty, and when Zhèng Yi eventually asked to marry her, Ching Shih only agreed if he would promise her a position of power in his organization as well as a share of the plunder. Without hesitation, the lovestruck Zhèng Yi agreed. Ching Shih proved to be a willing and eager protégé, and their marriage quickly evolved into a very lucrative, often deadly, partnership. Zhèng Yi taught her to how to command a crew, run a ship, and navigate the seas. Ching Shih had been around rough, dangerous characters before and, prior to meeting her pirate husband, had faced many precarious situations in her life. In short, she feared no man and took to the life of a pirate like a moth to flame.

While Zhèng Yi was content commanding a ragtag consortium of outlaws, his ambitious wife saw the potential for much greater things. She took to task organizing smaller pirate bands and bringing them under the banner of the Red Flag Fleet by enticing them with promises of larger payoffs and bigger shares of captured bounty. Ching Shih's aggressive plans paid off handsomely, and the Red Flag Fleet soon boasted a force of more than three hundred ships and almost 70,000 pirates.

Six years after their marriage, Zhèng Yi died, leaving his wife as the sole commander of the formidable pirate army. Zhèng Yi had been a loyal and crucial part of their burgeoning empire, but after his death Ching Shih's power only continued to flourish. She was ruthless but fair, strict but generous, and never reneged on her promises of spreading the wealth. Loot was shared equally among all of the pirate crews and anyone caught stealing or trimming from a pilfered cache of treasure was put to death. Ching Shih incorporated a brand of "frontier justice" among her followers: children and female captives were released unharmed, and anyone found abusing them faced severe disciplinary action. If a pirate wanted to take a captive as a wife, he had to do so under the strict rules and guidelines set forth by Ching Shih; it had to be consensual, and any married pirates who were unfaithful to their wives or did not take proper care of them risked execution.

Under Ching Shih's command, the Red Flag Fleet controlled the entire South China Sea and the pressure on the Chinese emperor grew with every ship that Ching

Shih captured and every piece of cargo, treasure, and spoil that her pirates stole. The ongoing raids, the ransacking of ships, and the disruption of trade along the shipping lanes and within coastal villages were beginning to affect the Chinese economy.

Other countries, as well as wealthy Chinese merchants and trading tycoons, started to demand a stop to Ching Shih's piratical activities. The emperor pitted his most experienced and accomplished military commanders against Ching Shih, only to see them fail time and time again. Military assistance from foreign powers was of little use against the Red Flag Fleet, and the desperate emperor watched the world's superpowers retreat in defeat.

It was, indeed, time to negotiate, but the emperor knew it wasn't going to be easy or pleasant.

During negotiations with the Chinese emperor, Ching Shih was bargaining from a position of strength and both she and the emperor knew it. Her demands were extreme, but there wasn't much the emperor could do about it. After several days of intense negotiating, Ching Shih was allowed to retire, promised a life free from capture or harassment from Chinese forces, and allowed to keep her ill-gained treasures—something unheard of at the time.

Ching Shih may have mellowed with age, but not much. After securing those extremely favorable conditions from a greatly relieved Chinese emperor, she retired from piracy, but the excitement that comes with an outlaw lifestyle beckoned again before long. She later opened a successful gambling house and brothel, adding to her already ample fortune.

In 1844, Ching Shih, the most powerful and successful pirate in history, died comfortably in bed, surrounded by loved ones at the age of sixty-nine.

# Princess Yennenga

*Even more than a war cry, I yearn to hear my own child's laughter.*

King Nedega, ruler of the Dagomba kingdom of the present day Northern Region of Ghana, was concerned and growing more nervous by the minute. Directly across from him, on the other side of the vast African plain just outside his territory, an army had gathered—and they hadn't shown up at his kingdom's doorstep just to say hello. The Malinke tribe was King Nedega's sworn enemy, and had been battling the mighty king and his people for many years. Seeing his enemies appear on the horizon wasn't unusual, and Nedega's troops had always fared well during the engagements, but this time, his most skilled and trusted military commander was nowhere to be seen. His soldiers waited patiently behind him, their weapons at the ready, awaiting his orders.

"Your three sons are in place and ready to move their respective battalions toward the Malinke forces at your command, your highness," one of Nedega's commanders reported. His three sons were fierce, respected warriors, and each commanded his own regiment. They were veterans of many battles against the Malinke soldiers as well as other enemy tribes, and were tough, reliable fighters. The king was extremely proud of his sons, but as skilled and dependable as they were, none were the king's most favored and experienced warrior leader. And until that warrior was located, the attack would have to wait.

"Where is Yennenga?" he screamed to his officers. "Where is my daughter?"

Princess Yennenga would appear eventually and lead her battalion of tribesmen into battle on that arid African plain, but she was mad at her father and he would have to wait. Yes, she was quite upset with him, and the king would have to sweat it out awhile longer before she appeared and led his army once again to victory.

Princess Yennenga had her first taste of battle at the tender age of fourteen, but she had come from a long line of warrior royalty, trained and eager to fight the Malinke since she was a young girl. Though her three older brothers quickly matured into formidable warriors and battalion leaders themselves, Yennenga stood out as being the most gifted warrior in the family. Her slim figure and beautiful face belied her fierce fighting expertise and superior warrior skills. She was a natural at horseback riding, and no man in her tribe could equal her deadly accurate javelin, spear, and bow marksmanship. Like her brothers, she was put in charge of her own battalion and usually went in first against enemy forces. She was both loyal and fiercely independent, and loved to fight. She derived particular pleasure decimating the armies of the Malinke, and her charge on horseback into advancing enemy soldiers inspired her men to drive forward into the fight, helping propel King Nedega's tribe to victory many times over.

Her desire to fight was soon overcome with a yearning to be a wife and a mother, and she pleaded with her father to let her find a husband and start a family. His answer was a resounding, "No." The princess was the very backbone of his military forces and he feared defeat if she retired from the battlefield. She loyally remained in military servitude to her father, but asked repeatedly for his permission to retire from the army so she could marry and bear children. His answer was always the same, and his patience with her request wore thin. She resorted to planting a field of wheat near her father's house and deliberately let it rot and die instead of harvesting it. Her father was confused and inquired about her irresponsible behavior.

"That wheat is me," replied the princess. "You are leaving me to die in the fields, alone, without a husband and children, just like the wheat."

It was a powerful and effective statement that both shamed and enraged the king. In his mind, his daughter had gone too far and he imprisoned her for her lack of respect.

He should have known such a punishment wouldn't be very effective.

With the help of a sympathetic tribesman, Princess Yennenga dressed as a man, stole a horse, and escaped under cover of darkness. While riding through the dense forests of Africa, the two were spotted and attacked by Malinke warriors. They fought fiercely and bravely, and though Yennenga managed to escape, her loyal companion was killed. She and her stallion nearly drowned while crossing a dangerous river, and, once they reached the safety of the other side, an exhausted Yennenga fell into a deep slumber on the back of her horse.

She eventually awakened and was startled to find herself looking into the curious eyes of a famed local elephant hunter named Riale. Though known for his expert hunting skills and strength, Riale was a kindhearted soul who took the strange but beautiful woman back to his village to rest. In the short time it took to nurse the fatigued and famished princess back to good health, Riale the elephant hunter and Yennenga the warrior had fallen deeply in love. They soon wed, and, true to her most cherished wishes, Yennenga bore a son and named him Ouedraogo, in honor of the trustworthy stallion she had ridden to escape her father. Ouedraogo became a renowned leader and king himself, famous for founding the formidable Mossi kingdom.

Yennenga lived almost a thousand years ago, but she is still venerated today in what is now Ouagadougou, Africa. In addition to streets and statues named in her honor, there is a prestigious African film award called the Yennenga Gold Stallion, which depicts the mighty princess warrior, spear in hand, astride a rearing war horse.

Though known for her prowess on the field of battle, Princess Yennenga finally achieved the name she cherished over any she had earned as a famed and fearless warrior: Yennenga, *Mother* of the Mossi.

# KUMANDER LIWAYWAY

*One of the things I am fighting for is the right to be myself.*

It was a split second of hesitation—and confusion—that cost the Japanese soldier his life. But he couldn't help it. He'd never seen anything so strange, so surreal, so... beautiful in all his life. At first glance, he thought she was a vision from heaven. She was stunning, and when he first spotted her staring at him in the dense Philippine jungle, he was mesmerized. Her hair was combed, coifed, and styled as though she were attending a formal ball, or even her own wedding. She wore ruby red lipstick that appeared freshly applied, the deep crimson hue offering a stark contrast against her beautiful pale face. The flourishing green foliage served as a frame for the striking goddess, and he continued to stare in immobilized amazement. She didn't appear afraid of him. In fact, she actually smiled.

"What is she doing out here?" he asked himself, still staring in awe at the vision before him. By the time she raised her cocked rifle and pointed it at him, the Japanese soldier knew full well what she was doing out there in that oppressively hot, bug-infested jungle. He figured it out rather quickly, but by then it was too late.

He was not the first Japanese soldier that Kumander Liwayway killed during the occupation of the Philippines during World War II, nor would he be the last. She was as lethal as she was beautiful, and the Japanese soldiers who fought against her would learn to fear the very sight of the deadly diva.

As a young child, Liwayway was like most girls growing up in her village; she liked playing with dolls, partaking in the traditional domestic duties that women were expected to perform in their communities at the time, and learning various beauty techniques. Liwayway took a particular interest in the latter, and she enjoyed experimenting with lipstick, gloss, beauty products, and a variety of hairstyles. She grew into a beautiful young girl and began entering and winning local beauty pageants. Her father, Basilio, was the mayor of their small village and Liwayway was the pride and joy of their family. It was a wonderful and peaceful time for her family and the village where they lived, and life was good.

Until the invasion.

The Japanese army arrived in the spring of 1939 and advanced so rapidly that resistance was minimal and attempts to fend off the invaders were futile. Repercussions for protestors were harsh, often resulting in torture and death. Though Basilio was a peaceful man, he and the other men in his village tried fighting back after the Japanese soldiers began a ruthless campaign of raping and killing the citizens of their village. After mounting a short but ineffective campaign of resistance, Basilio was caught by the Japanese, tortured, and publicly executed in the village square. Liwayway lay sobbing by her father's corpse as the smiling Japanese commandant who had just killed him, stepped over their bodies. The commandant looked down at the wailing girl and briefly thought about killing her, too, but passed on the idea. After all, what threat could a young girl like that possibly be?

It was a decision he would come to regret.

Liwaway joined the growing Philippine resistance movement and took to mastering weapons, jungle fighting techniques, and guerrilla warfare. Her skills developed quicker than most, and after proving herself against Japanese forces, she was soon designated chief of her own division. Her troops took to calling her Kumander Liwayway, and despite the harsh jungle conditions and difficult terrain, she always took care to apply makeup and have her hair styled before heading into battle. When asked about her insistence on looking so attractive while engaged in guerilla fighting, the former beauty queen simply replied, "One of the things I am fighting for is the right to be myself."

Her unit became a fierce, feared band of warriors, and her leadership abilities resulted in heavy losses for the Japanese. Liwayway particularly enjoyed stealing food and supplies from the Japanese, using their own purloined weapons against them. She was described as "a terror on the battlefield," and her determination to drive the occupiers from her country only magnified her deeply ingrained fortitude. During one battle, when the Japanese appeared to be gaining the upper hand, Liwayway's commander ordered a retreat. Liwayway refused his order and implored her men to stay and fight. Fight they did. They soon stopped the Japanese advance in its tracks and continued their onslaught until reinforcements arrived. The Philippine forces emerged victorious, and Liwayway and her unit were credited with turning the tide of the battle and very nearly defeating the enemy all on their own.

Her unit also earned the respect of the Allies after Liwayway and her resistance fighters rescued many downed British, Australian, and American pilots, providing them with protection as they guided them safely back to Allied lines.

While Liwayway embraced her femininity, she demanded respect and had the reputation and wherewithal to back it up. A fellow guerilla fighter, who continued making unwelcome sexual comments and advances toward Liwayway, soon found a pair of pistols trained on him by the very object of his desire.

"Are these gifts?" he asked, baffled by her intent.

"If you consider being shot to death a gift," she replied coldly. "Choose one."

She was openly challenging him to a duel in front of the rest of the unit. To refuse such a challenge—especially from a woman—would be a mark of great shame and dishonor. On the other hand, he knew all too well what the likely consequence would be should he take this lethal beauty up on her offer. The harasser turned bright red, backed down immediately, and slinked away, never uttering another disparaging word to her again.

After the war, Liwayway continued to fight, swapping her gun for a pen. She lobbied fiercely—and successfully—for the rights of female Philippine war veterans to secure pensions, and served as an advocate for the poor and mistreated until her death in 2014 at the age of ninety-five.

# ARTEMISIA I OF CARIA

*Above all other captains, she performed with the utmost bravery.*

Themistocles, the famed Athenian politician and general, preferred that the Persian commander be brought to him alive. If that weren't possible, however, he made it clear he would settle for the enemy's head on a spear. To demonstrate his sincerity, he offered a jaw-dropping reward of ten thousand drachmas to any of the Athenian captains under his command who succeeded in this task during the upcoming battle against their Persian rivals. One of most prominent and experienced captains in the entire Athenian navy was Ameinias. Though a captain of his stature lived an extravagant lifestyle—and enjoyed tremendous power and prestige among his peers—ten thousand drachmas was an enormous sum by any measure, and Ameinias vowed to collect the prize. He loved to fight, hated the Persians, and, despite the larger fleet assembled in the straits of Salamis, was eager to engage in what would likely be a final showdown between the two superpowers.

Originally dismissed as underdogs, Athens dominated the battle that day, unexpectedly routing their nemesis with a fleet far smaller than the opposing Persian force. Given that a Persian victory would have impeded Greek influence throughout the course of history, the Battle of Salamis was a monumental event that, arguably, altered the course of all mankind. While the battle itself was a historical achievement of epic proportions for that esteemed Greek state, the victory was somewhat bittersweet for Themistocles, Ameinias, and every other Greek captain who fought that day hoping to both defeat the Persians and collect a massive bounty.

Artemisia, the despised Persian commander, had escaped.

There were many reasons the Greek general was so determined to bring the elusive Artemisia to justice. She was an experienced naval commander and a formidable foe, with a well-earned reputation for cunning and ruthlessness. Artemisia was also a close and trusted advisor to Xerxes, the Persian king, who was actively trying to invade the fractured states of Athens and bring them under his subjugation. Even more significantly, Artemisia was a brilliant strategist with an almost prophetic ability to foresee crucial events before they unfolded. These were among the myriad reasons that Themistocles sought to entice his navy captains to capture the Persian commander and bring her to him in chains—or on a slab. But the predominant reason for his ire was that Artemisia had grievously offended the Greek battalion simply by being a woman.

Prior to the Battle of Salamis, the Greco-Persian Wars appeared to be drawing to an end, with victory well within reach for Xerxes and his Persian forces. When he assembled his top naval commanders to discuss strategy, it had been strongly proposed by most of his top brass that the Persian navy move forward with an aggressive campaign against the weakened and far smaller Athenian Greek navy in the Straits of Salamis, just off the coast of mainland Greece. Artemisia, however, found the maneuver entirely unnecessary, if not foolish, and wasn't hesitant to express her strong opposition to the plan.

"The Greeks are greatly weakened," she argued to the all-male staff. "We should wait them out. Why suffer the loss of a single Persian life when the enemy will eventually lay down their arms and return to Athens for wont of starving to death?"

Ironically, though Xerxes the Persian king openly extolled the advice of the wise and solitary female member of his trusted inner circle, it was her advice he chose to ignore. The Battle of Salamis was on.

Though staunchly opposed to the decision to engage the Greeks that day, Artemisia was a loyal and committed warrior and entered the fray with five Persian ships under her command. At best, a naval battle of such epic proportions in 440 B.C. could only be described as controlled chaos. The primary strategy of both sides involved ramming enemy vessels with the hope of sinking, disabling, or overwhelming the broadsided ship with a fusillade of arrows, spears, and flaming projectiles.

The straits were narrow to begin with, and with so many ships jockeying for position, the naval battle was pandemonium. From the start, things went very poorly for the overconfident Persians. In an attempt to blockade the Greeks, the Persian ships found themselves bottlenecked and defenseless at one end of the Straits of Salamis. Greek ships took quick advantage of the Persian blunder and fires soon broke out among the crush of jammed and sinking Persian vessels. Cries of agony pierced the smoke-filled air as Persian mariners perished en masse on the burning decks of their doomed vessels. The churning sea was awash in floating bodies and debris.

As the battle raged on, King Xerxes watched in horror from his perch on a cliff high above. The sole bright spot in the unfolding travesty was Artemisia and her crews, who expertly maneuvered their vessels away from the floundering cluster of doomed Persian ships. She darted deftly about the open water in the middle of the strait, sinking at least one enemy ship and damaging several others. A Greek warship began closing in on her, determined to decimate her ship and prevent her from inflicting further damage on the Athenian fleet. Artemisia soon found herself in the precarious position of being sandwiched between the ill-fated Persian fleet and the Greek ship bearing down her. There was little chance of escape.

Artemisia quickly ordered the Persian flag taken down from her topsail, and, in a display of ruthless cunning, proceeded to ram a friendly Persian ship. It was a bold if not potentially disastrous move, but this maneuver succeeded in confusing the Athenian captain into thinking Artemisia's ship was an ally. The Greek ship ceased its pursuit, enabling Artemisia to right her ship and rejoin the fight. The ambitious Greek captain never knew how close he had come to securing that coveted ten thousand drachma reward.

Despite the devastating defeat of his once invincible navy, Xerxes expressed his gratitude to Artemisia for her exemplary actions during the Battle of Salamis, and he commended her above all the other Persian captains who fought that day. He bestowed a gift of captured Athenian armor upon her and placed Artemisia in command of an even larger naval fleet. He never doubted her advice or questioned her guidance again, and confidently assigned a number of challenging and difficult military strategies to her.

Knowledge of her final years and death are unknown, though her profile has been found adorning coins from that long-ago era, solid proof that her contributions to king and country were greatly recognized and admired.

# Milunka Savic

*I will wait. To fight for my country, I will wait as long as it takes.*

The twenty-three Bulgarian soldiers were devastated. Not only were they now captives, it was but a single Serbian soldier who had charged their position, killed several of their comrades, and now held them all at gunpoint, marching them with hands above their heads toward Serbian lines. One of the Bulgarians couldn't contain his disgust any longer and spat into the dirt in front of him as he marched past the enemy soldier.

"Captured by one man!" he grumbled. "What could possibly be more humiliating?"

The Serb soldier chuckled and answered immediately, "Being captured by one woman?"

The Serb laughed aloud but only a few of those in the back of the long line of surrendering soldiers heard it. They turned and stared at the soldier whose gun was still trained on them. One had even stopped in his tracks and looked back, bewildered at the sound of the soldier's laugh. Was he crazy or had it sounded distinctly…female?

He wasn't crazy and it was just as well his comrades didn't know that the soldier who had single-handedly advanced upon their position and was now taking them prisoner was Milunka Savic, a female Serbian soldier.

Milunka Savic took to combat like a ravaged tiger to meat, and would end up fighting in three wars, becoming the single most decorated female warrior in history. Milunka's journey started the day her brother received his enlistment papers at the beginning of the First Balkan War. Perhaps to protect her younger sibling, as well as to do her part to defend her homeland, Milunka cut her hair short, dressed in men's attire, and enlisted in the army in place of her brother. The ruse worked and she soon found herself immersed in vigorous basic training alongside her unsuspecting fellow soldiers. She excelled in boot camp, standing out for both her leadership abilities and soldiering skills. She attained the rank of colonel without anyone guessing her true gender. With the war still raging between her fellow Serbs and their Bulgarian enemies, it didn't take long before she and her fellow recruits were rushed to the front.

She performed fearlessly during her first taste of battle, inflicting heavy casualties upon her Bulgarian enemies before being shot in the chest. While recovering from her wounds, Milunka's true identity came to light, but due to her extreme bravery and battlefield contributions, her superiors offered her a nursing position instead of punishing her.

Milunka refused.

"I am best suited to inflict wounds rather than to cure them," she responded curtly. When informed by her commanding officer that he would have to give long and serious thought before sending her into battle again, her answer was just as blunt. "I'll wait," she said, standing at attention like a true soldier. More than an hour later, the commander returned from his office to find Milunka still standing at rapt attention awaiting his answer. He not only acquiesced and agreed to send her back to the frontlines, but also promoted her to corporal.

It was a wise decision.

Milunka Savic's outstanding actions during her first battle would pale in comparison to her later acts of valor. While leading a charge across the dreaded "no man's land" between opposing enemy forces, she was blown into a ditch by an explosive and riddled with shrapnel. She crawled from the muddy trench, composed herself, then rallied her stalled comrades into continuing the charge until they overran the enemy forces, taking several prisoners.

While proficient in almost every weapon, Milunka's preference was the hand grenade. During the Second Balkan War, she led a charge against a Bulgarian force twice the size of her own. The devastating results of her accuracy in throwing the explosive projectiles in the ensuing victory earned her the nickname the "Bomber of Kolubara."

Milunka was discharged from military service with almost as many medals as scars. Her battlefield exploits are almost beyond belief, and were they not so well documented, they would defy plausibility. Over a span of seven years, Milunka fought in three wars on two continents and is still the most decorated female war veteran in all of history. She was honored and respected beyond her home country of Serbia, drawing praise and recognition from a host of grateful countries. Among other medals and commendations, she was awarded the Order of Karađorđe's Star (Serbia's highest military and civilian decoration), France's Légion d'honneur *twice* (the highest French order of merit for military and civil merits), the Croix de Guerre (France's high medal for heroism during combat), Russia's Cross of St. George, the British medal of the Most Distinguished Order of Saint Michael and Saint George, and Serbia's Medal of Miloš Obilić for bravery and valor in combat.

Milunka declined a generous offer from France that would have provided her with a decent pension and a comfortable existence, preferring instead to live in Belgrade. She slipped into obscurity for much of her later years and endured a number of hardships, including being sent to a concentration camp for not paying homage to the Nazis during World War II. Milunka married, divorced, raised one daughter, adopted three others, and worked a string of menial jobs. By the 1950s, the most decorated female warrior in history was still a Belgrade resident and living in abject poverty in a crumbling house.

Were it not for her last minute decision to attend a war veteran's jubilee celebration wearing her medals, Milunka and her incredible life story would have likely disappeared into the dusty annals of history. Several jubilee participants, including veterans and high-ranking officers, noticed her medals and engaged the seemingly harmless elderly woman in conversation. They were astonished by her history and the exploits she shared. News of her background soon spread, and public pressure built after her story was revealed in newspaper accounts. Her situation slowly improved and by 1972, she was living in a respectable apartment funded by the Belgrade government. She died in 1973 at the age of eighty-one in Belgrade, where a street is still named after her, a small but notable token of recognition for one of the bravest people in history.

# Queen Amanirenas

*I see more with one eye than all their legions see with two.*

Queen Amanirenas, ruler of the Kushite people, sat astride her large Nubian war stallion and studied the Egyptian valley below. She had recently lost an eye while battling the Roman army in that very same valley, and while the pain still troubled her, it was a comforting reminder that she was still alive, and that victory was near at hand. Behind her, the legion of mounted Kushite warriors under her command were also eager to engage the powerful, though floundering, Roman forces. Though Rome had recently conquered Egypt, the Kushite's northern neighbor, and had far superior numbers than the much smaller kingdom, Queen Amanirenas's tenacity, cunning, and brilliance—in both political and military matters—would bring Rome to heel.

The queen was all too familiar with Rome's insatiable thirst for power and knew that it would not stop at Egypt. She had the same maps as the Roman generals and knew well that the Kingdom of Kush was likely their next target. This imminent threat had prompted the Kushite queen to pull a highly unusual, extremely risky, and incredibly bold move—she attacked the Romans first. It was brazen, but likely one of the most brilliant military strategies in history.

Employing the element of surprise, the Kushites advanced quickly against the sparse Roman forces left guarding the newly conquered Egypt. Their victories were swift and decisive, capturing both the city of Syene and the territory of Philae. With lightning speed, the Kushite armies sacked the conquered territories of Egypt, taking prisoners, plunder, supplies, and loot. In the process, Queen Amanirenas and her army destroyed or defaced every statue and monument of Emperor Augustus that they found during the siege. In an added display of defiance, Queen Amanirenas had a bust of Augustus buried at the front gates of her palace so that all who entered would tread on the head of her enemy.

As expected, the Romans rapidly retaliated, laying waste to much of the Kushite land and killing its people. After recovering Syene and Philae, Augustus ordered that the Kushite capital be razed and any Kushite people captured either be slaughtered or enslaved.

While these kinds of vicious Roman tactics usually terrified a besieged population into submission, it only proved to infuriate Queen Amanirenas further. She responded by leading her Kushite army in a shocking counterattack, using war elephants against the Roman soldiers with devastating results. Queen Amanirenas proved as vicious and unpredictable as any foe the Romans had ever faced, personally feeding captured soldiers to her pet lions. She defied conventional military wisdom of the time and rarely paused to allow her army to recover from attacks. Her forces regrouped quickly and counterattacked with unrelenting aggression, giving the Roman forces little respite or rest between battles. The Kushite queen was as politically astute as she was strategically, and she could pinpoint vulnerabilities with uncanny precision. The Roman Empire had expanded too quickly, too radically, and revolts along its vast borders were increasing almost daily. In addition to the problems springing up on the outskirts of the empire, Rome was also experiencing a surge of conflicts and uprisings from within. This combination of internal and external strife was straining the already stretched military resources, and the Roman army was reaching a breaking point.

Unfortunately for Rome, Queen Amanirenas was well aware of all of this. She was a masterful military strategist, and the Romans soon found themselves locked in an expensive and bloody stalemate with the wily queen and her small but determined army. Despite having superior numbers and weaponry, the Romans faced an unusually resilient foe hell-bent on achieving what was thought to be an impossible task—defeating the Roman army. They threw everything they had at her, but the Kushite queen showed no signs of giving up.

After five long years, the Romans had had enough, and in a rare display of acquiescence, Emperor Augustus called for negotiations. Roman officials made staunch assurances that if the Kushites remained within their borders and promised not to attack Egypt again, they would respond in kind. This was the outcome Queen Amanirenas had sought from the outset. Her initial attack and foray into Egypt was a ploy; she had no designs on Rome's northern territory—her aggression had been a strategy of "the best defense is a good offense," a deterrent against any future Roman plans to encroach upon her kingdom. It was a long, bloody, nightmarish gamble that paid off for the Kushite queen and her subjects. When the Nubians and Romans finally entered into negotiations, the defiant queen snubbed the Romans one last time by sending mediators in her place to meet August Caesar. The resultant treaty was entirely favorable to the Nubians, with Rome even waiving its normal demand for taxes. The Romans departed Queen Amanirenas's territory and never returned.

Queen Amanirenas and her army fought so fiercely and so successfully that Roman forces never again moved beyond Egypt. Queen Amanirenas continued to rule the Kushite people and her reputation as a fierce and fearless warrior lingered long into her reign. Alexander the Great entertained thoughts of crossing into Kushite territory, but after consulting with his military advisors he wisely thought the better of it. Like the Roman army before him, Alexander amassed his enormous forces on the Kushite border and tried to intimidate the queen into capitulating. She gathered her own forces and faced him astride her war horse, not only refusing to bow to his demands to surrender, but beckoning him forth to fight. Rather than face heavy losses against the fearless warrior queen, Alexander chose to take a longer, albeit safer route to his intended destination.

Due to Queen Amanirenas' policies and rule, the Kushites lived in relative peace and prosperity for the next three hundred years.

# GRACE O'MALLEY

*The most notorious woman on all the western coasts and the nurse of all rebellions for forty years.*

Sir Richard Bingham, the Englishman who was appointed governor of County Connacht, Ireland, was losing patience. In fact, he'd had more than enough of Grace O'Malley, the so-called "Pirate Queen of Ireland," whose power, wealth, and influence was growing unimpeded not only in Connacht, but throughout the Emerald Isle, as well. It was time to rein her in—kill her, if necessary—and confiscate her vast holdings of cattle, horses, ships, castles, weapons, and food stores. Governor Bingham had conspired with the local sheriff, offering the unscrupulous lawman a share of the spoils once they laid waste to O'Malley and her followers. With a large group of armed men under their command, they moved forward under the cover of darkness and began the siege.

It was a short fight.

The attackers who weren't killed trying to storm the castle fled, beaten and bloody, into the surrounding countryside, and the governor and sheriff barely escaped with their lives.

The governor should have known not to underestimate his foe; the Pirate Queen came from a long line of fierce fighters, and her clan's propensity for violence was well established in Ireland and beyond. Her father had been a feared and respected Irish lord, known for his combat agility on both land and sea. The O'Malley clan constructed a row of castles along the coastline and its ships patrolled the ocean off the Connacht shore, "taxing" all those who fished or traveled in what was deemed its territory—including English ships. Though she had a brother, when Grace's father passed away, it was the Pirate Queen who assumed control of the family dynasty, not him. It was a wise transition, and Grace proved to be even more successful than her father in expanding the family enterprise.

Life on the seas off the Irish coast could be even more lawless than on land, and piracy was a concern for anyone who chose to work or travel by boat. Even a fearsome seafaring clan like the O'Malleys wasn't invulnerable to attack by the plentiful and nefarious maritime thieves found patrolling the waters—though attacking a craft under the command of the Pirate Queen was never a mistake that was made twice. Her sloop was once stormed by a band of Turkish pirates a day after she gave birth to her son aboard ship. Irate at being disturbed, Grace O'Malley leapt from her bunk, grabbed two short flintlock rifles, and strode furiously onto the deck. Before the Turkish pirates could announce their intentions to take her ship, O'Malley blasted the two Turkish officers in charge with the flintlocks and proceeded to take control of the pirate ship and its entire crew. She then berated her own crew for allowing her nap to be interrupted and went back to bed below deck.

After her first husband was ambushed and killed by a rival Irish clan, Grace found love again with a shipwrecked sailor living in Connacht. Tragically, he, too, was murdered by a rival family known as the MacMahon clan of Doona. This time, the Pirate Queen wasn't going to let the offense go unanswered and set to work seeking revenge. O'Malley led a band of warriors into the MacMahon castle, slew her boyfriend's killers, sacked the place, and added another castle to her collection. Along with the castle, the Pirate Queen also earned another nickname: "The Dark Lady of Doona."

O'Malley and her loyalists became so successful and so brazen in their attacks on English ships and merchants that the crown finally mounted a coordinated attack on her castles and ships. Once again, the Pirate Queen made short work of the aggressors and sent them scurrying back to England in defeat.

O'Malley's growing influence and expanding control continued to infuriate her lifelong enemy, the humiliated Governor Bingham. Unable to defeat the fierce warrior queen in battle, he opted instead to have her two sons and stepbrother kidnapped and sent back to England in chains. It was an ill-considered and outrageous maneuver, for Governor Bingham neglected to account for the fact that Grace O'Malley was as educated and intelligent as she was ruthless. Maintaining her composure, Grace O'Malley immediately petitioned the English queen for a meeting to discuss the situation. Despite the strong opposition of Governor Bingham, Queen Elizabeth granted her the meeting, and O'Malley set sail for England to negotiate for her family's freedom. The Pirate Queen was as shrewd as she was tough, and made sure to greet the English queen wearing her finest gown and jewelry.

The meeting began on an uncomfortable note when Grace O'Malley, refusing to recognize Elizabeth as the Queen of Ireland, declined to bow. Queen Elizabeth couldn't speak Gaelic, and Grace O'Malley knew no English, so the two educated female leaders conversed in Latin. A guarded but reciprocal respect grew between the lady leaders, and Elizabeth soon agreed to O'Malley's appeal that her family be freed and she be allowed to maintain control of her holdings. In a final coup d'etat, O'Malley demanded the removal of Bingham as Governor of Connacht—which the English queen also agreed to. Satisfied enough with the negotiations, O'Malley sailed home to Ireland with her sons and stepbrother in tow.

Though the agreement between the Pirate Queen and the English monarch was indeed an historical accomplishment, the truce didn't last long; despite her pledge to Grace O'Malley, Queen Elizabeth reappointed Bingham as governor of O'Malley's lands. It was a grave miscalculation on Elizabeth's part, and the fiery Irish warlord reacted in kind. Leveraging her vast network of pirates, smugglers, highwaymen, and rebellious Irish clans, O'Malley fired up an insurgency that attacked English troops, plundered their ships, and disrupted commerce on both land and sea. Grace O'Malley was a formidable and constant thorn in the side of the English for more than forty years, and was never once captured or imprisoned.

Ironically, Grace O'Malley, the infamous Pirate Queen of Ireland passed away in 1603, the very same year that her nemesis across the water, Queen Elizabeth, died.

# KHUTULUN

*Khutulun was a superb warrior, unlike any I've ever seen.*

He was nervous until he saw his opponent. The wrestler from the rival Mongolian clan was far smaller than he had expected, and he allowed himself to relax a bit. He was bigger, stronger, undefeated, and now envisioned a quick victory. Still, there was a lot at stake and he tried to stay focused on his opponent, who was staring fearlessly into his eyes from across the clearing. Along with archery and horseback riding, wrestling was an almost sacred activity to the Mongols, one of the "Three Manly Skills" held sacrosanct in that warrior culture.

The wrestler he was pitted against from the rival tribe was also undefeated, and the frenzied excitement in the massive crowd of Mongolian spectators bordered on mayhem. Substantial wagers were being placed for the combatants, who slowly circled one another. Along with the title of champion wrestler of the entire Mongolian empire, the victor would be awarded one hundred of the rival clan's finest horses, a chest plate adorned in gold, and a bow and arrow set made from the finest craftsmen in all of Asia. But the crown jewel to the Mongolian warrior, who now bore down upon his diminutive rival, would be the taking of a new bride as part of his winnings.

He might have prevailed if he had feigned left instead of right, or if he had swept his right foot forward and taken the smaller Mongolian warrior to the ground. As it was, he ended up facedown in the dirt, with his arm twisted behind his back. The roar from the crowd was deafening and by the time he struggled to his feet, he had lost the first match of his career along with a hundred of his clan's prized horses. He scanned the crowd in search of his victorious opponent, but the victor had already been raised onto the shoulders of the jubilant tribe and marched off toward a raucous feast to celebrate the victory.

Despite the Mongolian warrior's humiliation at his defeat, there was little shame, even in a testosterone-fueled culture like the Mongols, of being overpowered and brought to heel by Khutulun, the female wrestling champion and renowned warrior of the Kaidu Khan tribe. Khutulun was the great-great-granddaughter of Genghis

Khan, founder and original ruler of the Mongolian Empire. Warrior blood ran through her veins like rivers through a mountain, and she remained undefeated in the wrestling ring until the day she died. She was so confident in her abilities that she offered a standing bet of one hundred horses—an enormous sum—to anyone who could beat her. As an added incentive, she boldly offered her hand in marriage as part of the champion's winnings. It was an enticing addition to an already enormous jackpot, and the strongest, most skilled wrestlers from throughout the vast Mongolian empire arrived to take her up on her daring challenge.

By the time she retired from wrestling, she had amassed a fortune of more than 10,000 horses—and no husband. In addition to her legendary accomplishments in the ring, Khutulun excelled in the other "Three Manly Skills" of archery and horseback riding.

Though her great-great-grandfather had created the largest contiguous empire in history, by the time Khutulun was born, the once unified Khan Dynasty had become fractured. Rivalries from within the empire had splintered into battling factions, leading to a tumult of civil wars. A bitter conflict between Khutulun's father, Kaidu, and his own uncle, Kublai Khan, crippled the empire for more than thirty years. Though Kaidu had fourteen sons—all capable and respected warriors in their own right—it was his daughter, Khutulun, upon whom he relied most for military and political advice. She was extremely savvy and understood the delicate intricacies of inner tribal politics. On the battlefield, she was as relentless and uncompromising as she was in the wrestling ring.

Though her archery talents were impressive, her most notable and awe-inspiring talent was her ability to ride headlong into battle on her war horse, snatch an enemy soldier with one hand, and carry the prisoner kicking and screaming back to her line, all while maintaining full control of her steed.

Marco Polo, the famous Italian explorer and merchant, personally witnessed Khutulun's legendary fighting talents during his travels to Asia. Though he had traveled extensively and witnessed many amazing things during his journeys, Marco Polo had never seen anyone quite like the Mongolian woman warrior.

"Like a hawk grabbing a chicken," he wrote in astonishment, explaining her unique ability to pluck larger enemies from the field of battle and carry them off. "Khutulun was a superb warrior, unlike any I've ever seen."

The prospect of a female warrior kidnapping significantly larger foes in the midst of a battling horde of fierce Mongolian warriors was enough to demoralize most enemies, especially in a culture as testosterone-fueled as Mongol society.

The next time Khutulun set her eyes on a warrior she wanted to pursue, she had no intention of dragging him off; the ferocious Mongolian fighter had fallen in love. Knowing the object of her affections could never beat her in the ring, she announced her retirement from wrestling and married him. She remained an indispensable figure in her father's inner circle, and toward the end of his life, Kaidu attempted to break with tradition and appoint Khutulun as the first female leader of a Mongolian clan. Though his daughter could physically whip any of them in the ring, the clan elders refused to even consider having a woman run the roost, and Khutulun's appointment was soundly denied. After Kaidu's death, Khutulun loyally guarded his tomb until she passed away five years later. Her fabled record as undefeated champion inspired modern Mongolian wrestling attire, designed with an open chest to ensure that both grapplers are male—and have a fair chance of winning!

# Nancy Wake

*I was never afraid. I was too busy to be afraid.*

The woman was an unusual but welcome sight, and the lone German soldier, cigarette dangling from his lips, stepped from his sentry box into the road. She was riding a bicycle and cruised to a wobbly stop when he put his hand up, motioning for her to dismount. She didn't appear at all nervous, and so he felt no immediate danger. His gun was still slung over his shoulder by its strap when he stepped toward her.

"Hello there," she said, smiling warmly.

He was dead before he even hit the ground, and never felt the fatal judo chop the mystery woman delivered to his throat. By the time his comrades found him cold and stiff by the side of the road, the lethal beauty who took his life was long gone.

Nancy Wake, the seemingly harmless woman who had sent the young German soldier to an early grave, wasn't afraid of much. Born in New Zealand and raised in Australia, the future espionage expert and decorated war hero was the youngest of six children and had always had a sense of adventure. Her wanderlust prompted her to leave home at sixteen years of age with a mere £200 to her name and travel to New York City. From New York, she ventured to London, where she developed a passion for journalism. She dedicated her time to learning the craft of writing and journalistic studies, eventually landing a job with Hearst newspapers. Her newfound career enabled her to travel throughout Europe, and it was in Vienna in the late 1930s, during Hitler's rise to power, that she first witnessed the brutality of Nazi youth gangs.

A few short years later, she was married and living in Marseille, France, when Hitler's German forces invaded her adoptive city. The deep loathing she felt for the Nazis intensified, and she quickly volunteered as an ambulance driver for the French Resistance. As a result of her mobility and her knowledge of the surrounding terrain, Nancy became an undercover courier and active participant in the French guerrilla movement. Her activities soon caught the attention of the Gestapo, who tapped her phones, read her mail, and monitored her whereabouts. After being tipped off that the Gestapo had issued a warrant for her arrest, Nancy Wake successfully eluded capture numerous times. The Nazis dubbed her the "White Mouse," and it wasn't long before Nancy Wake was listed as the most wanted person in the Marseille region, with a bounty of five million francs on her head. After several close calls, the Resistance ordered her back to England, where Nancy Wake began intense training under a newly formed and highly secretive British special operations group called the Special Operations Executive (SOE). She proved to be a spectacular student. Observing her during training, one of Wake's female instructors noted, "She's a real Australian bombshell, that one. And everything she does, she does well; she's a very good, very fast shot, and puts the men to shame by her cheerful spirit and strength of character."

Nancy Wake mastered the fine arts of espionage, sabotage, and every other manner of guerilla warfare, and soon found herself parachuting back into France doing what she loved most—assisting the French Resistance in making life as miserable as possible for the Nazis.

She did not disappoint.

Nancy Wake spent the rest of the war wreaking havoc in every way known to man—and woman. She blew up bridges, destroyed railroads, disrupted German supply lines, conducted raids, and saved the lives of hundreds of Allied soldiers and downed airmen by escorting them safely through German occupied territory. She also killed lots of Nazis along the way. During one battle, Nancy Wake and a group of 7,000 French Resistance fighters found themselves facing more than 20,000 German troops. Under Nancy Wake's guidance and expertise, what could well have been a disaster turned into a great victory for the Resistance fighters. The French guerrillas slaughtered the Germans, killing almost 1,500 while losing only 100 of their own.

On another mission, Nancy Wake coordinated guerrilla forces in a daring night raid against Gestapo headquarters, where she and her comrades killed thirty-eight enemy soldiers and high-ranking Nazi officers.

One Resistance fighter said of Wake, "She is the most feminine woman I know—until the fighting starts. Then she is like five men."

It was only at the war's end that she learned her beloved husband had been tortured and killed by the Nazis for refusing to divulge her whereabouts. Wake returned to England and continued her work as an intelligence officer, eventually marrying again. After many years of loyal service, she and her second husband moved to Australia, where Wake toyed with politics and wrote a bestselling book about her life called *The White Mouse.*

Her wartime exploits earned her an astounding collection of medals from a number of countries, including the George Cross (United Kingdom), the Medal of Freedom (United States), Médaille de la Résistance (France), and she was the three-times recipient of the French Croix de Guerre. In addition, Nancy Wake was presented with New Zealand's RSA Badge in Gold, as well as made a Companion of the Order of Australia, an honor bestowed upon Australian citizens for meritorious service.

Nancy Wake lived a hardy ninety-eight years and died on August 7, 2011. She requested her ashes be spread in her beloved France where she had lived, loved, and fought.

# Agustina de Aragón

*I will rest when Spain lies with me on freedom's bed.*

She brought apples, not bullets, but the defenders of the Spanish city of Zaragoza were grateful anyway. They were a ragtag bunch of volunteers consisting primarily of farmers, tradesmen, peasants, and average townsfolk—hardly a match for Napoleon's battle-hardened army. Their food stocks were alarmingly low, and the sight of Agustina de Aragón, the petite woman bearing a basketful of the succulent red ripe fruit, seemed almost miraculous.

"Bless you, angel!" the Spanish commander exclaimed, grabbing a large apple and biting into it ravenously. "You are braver than you are kind, and you are most certainly kind!"

Agustina deposited the load of precious fruit onto the muddy ground and was immediately swarmed by a mass of her tattered, famished countrymen who eagerly devoured the apples on the spot. Agustina was shocked at the state of the town. The ramparts were littered with dead bodies; the screams and moans of others who were wounded and dying were horrifying to hear. Deafening explosions and rifle fire shook the earth and filled the air with the acrid smell of gunpowder.

She had always known Zaragoza to be peaceful and picturesque. It was, after all, a city that hadn't seen war in more than four hundred years. But this was 1808, and Napoleon's march across Spain had culminated in the siege of Zaragoza, the only city left in Northern Spain not yet conquered by the power-hungry French general. Agustina had always been fascinated by the military and had demonstrated a keen interest in weaponry and battlefield strategy as a young girl. She even married an artillery gunner, who regaled her with stories of a life of battle and soldiery. Nothing, however, prepared her for what she witnessed on the walls of Zaragoza. As she stood, aghast at the carnage, a barrage of French cannon fire destroyed a nearby rampart, knocking Agustina to her feet. The French forces surged forward, slaughtering the Spanish defenses with their bayonets as they lay wounded on the ground. Chaos prevailed as the untrained and demoralized Spanish defenders fled for their lives.

The Spanish commander seized Agustina's arm and urged her to flee, but she shook him off. "Run, Agustina!" he implored. "Save yourself!"

Agustina was oblivious to his entreaties. She stood alone on the rampart, staring in horror as she witnessed the slaughter of women and children by the attacking French forces.

She had seen enough, had enough, and her horror turned to a blind rage.

Agustina ran forward, toward the carnage, toward the enemy, toward certain death. She made it to an abandoned Spanish cannon battery, and, using all her strength, turned the cannon toward the advancing French forces, the vanguard of which were then just yards away from her position. She lit the fuse and was knocked backward when the cannon fired point blank into a swarm of French soldiers making their way over the ramparts. Agustina jumped to her feet and frantically began loading the cannon for a second assault. The stunned French soldiers weren't the only ones that day to stare in amazement as the lone Spanish woman fired the cannon into their midst; her fleeing countrymen, inspired by her courage, halted their retreat. Spanish defenders surged toward the fight, and the French were quickly driven back by the reinvigorated Spanish. Agustina's actions turned the tide of the battle, and the city of Zaragoza remained free for several more weeks.

After her incredible heroics that day, Agustina became committed to driving the French invaders entirely out of Spain, and continued to engage in active combat roles. Eventually, her luck ran out and she was captured by the French. If the enemy had hoped to keep its female nemesis safely under lock and key, it was greatly disappointed. Agustina successfully mounted a daring escape and was soon back in the fight. She joined Spanish rebel forces and engaged in a series of ambushes, sabotage, and other guerilla activities meant to harass and demoralize French troops. She later proved an invaluable military asset in several campaigns, fighting with the allies against Napoleon. Agustina served valiantly as a frontline battery commander with the British, and fought in the campaigns that finally drove the French from her beloved Spanish soil.

After the war, she married a doctor and lived a relatively quiet and respectable life. In later years, she could be spotted taking walks about the city, proudly displaying her many medals and chatting with anyone curious enough to inquire about them. She lived until the ripe age of seventy-one, her wartime exploits inspiring numerous paintings, sketches, poems, books, and films.

# KITTUR RANI CHENNAMMA

*This Indian warrior queen didn't just fight the British; she defeated them, too!*

The name British East India Company sounds innocuous enough, but the corporate moniker belied a dark history wrought with sinister motives and a blood-soaked past. While the company was formed to engage in world trade, its growth strategies would ultimately depend on global colonialization and conquest. Commerce in cotton, silk, dyes, salt, spices, and tea soon expanded to include slavery and opium. As a land rich in people and resources, India found itself in the unenviable position of being one of the most highly sought-after prizes for the British East India Company. By the early 1800s, the organization was firmly entrenched in India, its policies proving disastrous for citizenry and land alike.

India consisted of a complex quilt of religions, classes, castes, tribes, and clans. Already separated into hundreds of different territories known as vassal or "princely states," India proved to be fertile ground for the type of divide-and-conquer strategy that had been used to fatten the coffers of the East India Company for hundreds of years. Through an ongoing campaign of broken promises, treachery, and military might, the British East India Company was intent upon realizing its goal of the complete subjugation of the Indian people and their country.

While there had been sporadic uprisings from an increasingly embittered population, the British forces, along with the private army of the British East India Company, had managed to subdue the insurgencies. The master plan of eventual—and complete—domination of India was moving forward.

The company had lots of plans, in fact.

But none of them involved dealing with a fiery Indian princess and warrior named Rani Chennamma, also known as the Queen of Kittur.

In 1824, Kittur Chennamma, as she is formally known, was head of the princely state of Kittur in Southern India. When the British East India Company used a deceptive ploy to try to annex Kittur—as it had successfully done many times before—it was entirely unprepared for her response. The treachery, shady dealings, and refusal to respect the sacred traditions of India's diverse cultures had finally resulted in outright conflict. Led by St. John *Thackeray*, an agent and collector for the British East India Company, the British forces gathered outside the fortified town where Rani and her compatriots were gathered, nervously preparing for battle. In addition to the annexation of her territory for his notorious employer, Thackeray also intended to confiscate Kittur's vast collection of treasure and jewels for himself. He had reason to be confident in a quick resolution with minimal resistance—he was leading a force of more than 20,000 soldiers backed up by almost 500 cannon. Thackeray would not have been nearly so complacent if he had known what was happening inside the fortified town.

Brandishing her sword above her head, Rani Chennamma stood on a platform before her nervous troops. The Queen of Kittur was calm, determined, and very, very angry.

"Today is the decisive day in the history of the Kittur kingdom. It is left to you to bring victory and glory to your motherland. We must all teach Thackeray and his soldiers a lesson they will never forget." The cheers from the revitalized Kittur troops echoed over the walls, unnerving the British. Sooner thereafter, the gates of Kittur swung open, and a charge of mounted Kittur soldiers, their deadly swords glittering in the hot sun, poured out to meet their British enemies. Rani Chennamma, the Queen of Kittur, sat astride a large stallion on the ramparts of the town, guiding her soldiers from above and watching as they decimated the British troops.

It was a moment that Rani Chennamma had inadvertently been preparing for all her life. Though born into a small village, she had received an education in martial arts, hunting, languages, sword fighting, and archery. She was an eager student and excelled in her pursuits, earning a reputation as an adventurous and brave girl. When she was just fifteen years old, a man-eating tiger terrorized nearby villages, killing a young boy who had been playing outside his house. With her bow slung over one shoulder, Rani Chennamma ventured into the forest to hunt the tiger down. She correctly surmised that the ferocious beast would stop by a nearby stream for a drink—and when it did just that, she slew it with a single arrow.

Rani Chennamma's bravery, fighting spirit, loyalty, and strategic acumen all culminated on that day in 1824 when she gave her speech, mounted her stallion, and directed her troops against the blaze of British guns. Thackeray, the overconfident field agent and leader of the British East India Company, fell early in the fight, along with several other British officers. It was an unexpected rout for Kittur Rani Chennamma, and her followers' cheers filled the sky around her as the humiliated British forces beat a hasty retreat. Two high-ranking British officers had been taken prisoner during the fight and were used as bargaining chips during subsequent negotiations.

While the British regrouped and returned with larger forces that eventually defeated Rani Channamma, the unexpected 1824 defeat of the occupying British forces served to further fuel the Indian drive for independence. Despite her capture and imprisonment, she continued her revolutionary fight against the British and the notorious British East India Company. In addition to attempting multiple escapes, she directed insurgencies and uprisings from her confinement and promoted the cause of Indian independence until the day she died on February 21, 1829.

Rani Channamma is celebrated in India today as the first female freedom fighter of the country. Appropriately enough, Pratibha Devisingh Patil, the first female president of India, unveiled a statue of the Queen of Kittur in 2007 in the Indian Parliament.

# Anne Bonny and Mary Read

*If you had fought like a man, you needn't be hanged like a dog!*

British naval captain Jonathan Barnet steered his pirate hunting sloop, *Snow-Tyger,* quickly toward the floundering ship he had just riddled with a volley of cannon fire off the coast of Jamaica. Captain Barnet had been in dogged pursuit of John "Calico Jack" Rackham and his pirate ship *William,* and it looked like his determination and hard work had finally paid off. Not only was the ship all but dead in the water, but the entire pirate crew of the *William,* including Calico Jack, had fled below deck—except for three brave buccaneers who refused to quit the fight.

"I demand all men aboard your ship give up!" Barnet hollered to the three pirates who remained fighting.

"Most have!" screamed back one of the pirates, shooting a flintlock pistol toward the *Snow-Tyger.* Captain Barnet ducked as the ball of lead whizzed past his head. Despite the battle raging around him, something about the pirate's voice caught his attention. Brandishing a sword in one hand and a flintlock pistol in the other, the swashbuckling outlaw presented a most fearsome figure. His voice, however, seemed curiously high-pitched, almost as if he were…a woman.

Before Captain Barnet could make sense of this strange occurrence, he witnessed yet another baffling incident on the deck of the *William.* The second of the three pirates raced toward the hold of the *William* and shouted below at his cowering shipmates, "If there's a man among ye, ye'll come up and fight like the man ye are to be!" When not a single comrade responded, the enraged pirate fired a shot down into the hold, killing one of the crew. The pirate's murderous tactic worked, and seconds later a horde of armed and screaming pirates emerged from below decks to join their three shipmates battling for their lives on the smoking deck of the *William.* While the crew of the *Snow-Tyger* responded with another volley of cannon fire, Captain Barnet once again found himself distracted, this time because the *second* pirate had also sounded distinctly…female.

The pirate vessel eventually succumbed to Captain Barnet, and the surviving

91

buccaneers were taken prisoner. While interrogating the captured outlaws, Barnet and his crew made a startling discovery—the two pirates that fought so aggressively on deck were, in fact, female; Anne Bonny and Mary Read's lives as bloodthirsty, fearless pirates on the high seas had come to an end.

Bonny and Read's upbringings had been remarkably similar; both were illegitimate and dressed as boys at an early age to pass off as "sons." Read was born and raised in England, and Bonny was from County Cork, Ireland. Both were described as hellions in their youth, difficult to control and prone to trouble. They were close in age, and may have actually lived in London at the same time, though they didn't meet in person until years later when both were disguised as men and working as pirates under the command of Calico Jack. Read had no father figure to speak of, while Bonny's father was a loving presence who did everything in his power to keep his daughter from taking a bad path in life. His later success as a prosperous businessman would eventually save his rebellious daughter's life.

Prior to her days as a pirate, Read, while still dressing as a man, joined the British military and fought with distinction during the Nine Years' War.

Though some people of that time were forced into an outlaw life after being taken prisoner or threatened with death by their captors, both Bonny and Read willingly joined the pirate life. By all accounts, they excelled at their chosen profession and were feared and respected by those who knew them. Anne Bonny beat one hapless fellow within an inch of his life after he groped her, and the randy scalawag spent nearly a month recovering from his wounds. Bonny and Read became close friends even before discovering one another's true gender, and their bond only strengthened when the truth became known.

Contrary to many historical accounts of piracy, pirate culture could actually be quite democratic. Captains could be voted out of power, plundered loot was expected to be distributed fairly, and crews were often extremely diverse, consisting of people from all manner of backgrounds, races, and origins. That being said, female pirates at the time were exceptionally rare, so it was no surprise that Captain Barnet was more than a little shocked to discover that the two toughest outlaws putting up the fiercest fight that day were women.

While a pirate might expect some semblance of democratic equality in his or her life aboard ship, the punishments meted out for such a life were also applied equally to all. Bonny and Read, along with the rest of their shipmates, were arrested, placed on trial for the crime of piracy, and sentenced to hang. Dorothy Thomas, a witness at the trial, had been captured by Rackham's crew and held prisoner for a time. According to Thomas's testimony, Bonny and Read, "dressed as men, fought with pistols and machetes like any other pirate, and were twice as ruthless."

As luck would have it, however, both women were soon discovered to be "quick with child." While most of their shipmates were executed as scheduled, Bonny and Read were spared the hangmen's noose because of their pregnancies and sentenced instead to lengthy prison terms.

Details of their whereabouts after their brush with the hangman are somewhat sketchy, though it's generally accepted that Mary Read died of fever while still in prison. It's believed that her "sister-in-arms," Anne Bonny, was eventually released, probably as a result of a bribe by her heartbroken father. Accounts of Bonny's life after her release vary; one story details her reconciliation with her wealthy father, while another claims she remarried and moved to the Bahamas, where she lived and died in relative obscurity. A third account describes her return to piracy dressed as a man, and her resumption of swashbuckling, lawless ways under another name. Based on Bonny's notorious history, it's not a very farfetched theory at all!

# DAHOMEY'S WOMEN WARRIORS

*Give a dog a bone and he will break it and eat. So will we do with the cities of the enemy.*

The Yorùbá tribe had taken the port city from its bitter enemies, the people of the Dahomey kingdom, and some of the younger Yorùbá fighters wanted to celebrate. The battle for the port had been quick and relatively easy, and these less experienced warriors were enjoying a self-congratulatory moment. They were both surprised at the light resistance offered by their Dahomean enemies, as well as impressed with what they saw as their own superiority on the field of battle. The older, wiser Yorùbá warriors, however, found no such comfort in the victory. The Dahomean force guarding the port was made up entirely of men, a factor that greatly troubled the seasoned Yorùbá veterans. An elder Yorùbá commander scanned the horizon before him, fixated on a distant dust cloud that was slowly approaching their position. A younger warrior, beaming with pride, walked up and stood next to him.

"The Dahomean men were no match for us," he bragged.

"No, they were not," agreed the commander solemnly. "But it's not the Dahomean men I am worried about."

With that, he squinted toward the dust cloud that was approaching across the dry African terrain. It could have been the scourging winds of a tornado or cyclone, but as it came nearer, he could see the sun flashing off the dreaded double-edged swords, known to cut men clean in two, and he could hear the rhythmic chants and the pounding beat of drums. There was indeed a Dahomean force coming back to reclaim the port from the Yorùbá, but this time it wasn't the men who had come to fight.

"They are here!" bellowed the chief, unable to disguise the terror in his voice. "The women have returned!"

The brazen young Yorùbá warriors would soon learn what had struck such fear into the hearts of their mentors.

While the history of the Dahomey Amazons almost borders on mythical, they were a very real, extremely lethal elite group of 6,000 fighters considered to be the first all-female frontline in modern history.

The Dahomey Amazons were the most feared fighting force along the Atlantic coast of Africa. The Dahomey kingdom was also known as "Black Sparta" due to its disciplined lifestyle and warrior culture. Despite being frequently outnumbered by its enemies, the Dahomey kingdom was just as frequently victorious in battle due to these women warriors. They found their origins in a renowned group of all-female elephant hunters, notorious for their fearless hunting techniques. Impressed with their skills, King Gezo, the Dahomean ruler, soon employed them as his personal bodyguards, eventually transforming them into the most deadly and disciplined unit of his armed forces. They were trained to be impervious to pain and hurled themselves into and over walls of thorny acacia bushes during military exercises. As further testament to their ability to withstand great pain, these almost superhuman women would don the acacia belts as badges of honor, the sharp thorns perpetually digging deep into their exposed flesh.

In addition to their own distinct uniforms, the Dahomean female warriors were armed with muskets, clubs, knives, and other weapons normally reserved for their male counterparts. Among those they were known for wielding with deadly accuracy was a dreaded two-sided sword capable of cutting a human in half. The Dahomean warriors were trained to never show fear, and retreat was never an option. It was understood by both friend and foe alike that the Dahomean women warriors fought to the death. In addition to arms training, battlefield strategy, and survival skills, these black Amazons were conditioned to be absolutely merciless to their enemies. As part of what was called their "insensitivity training," they were directed to execute hapless male prisoners, often by tossing them over the high walls of the king's palace. The only thing worse than being slain in battle by a Dahomean warrior was the prospect of being taken alive.

While non-combatant women in Dahomean society lived a more restricted life, their female warrior counterparts enjoyed high status, unattainable by even the men of the tribe. They rose to positions of influence and prominence, serving on councils where their voices and opinions regarding tribal issues and policy were heard. Being a part of the king's most trusted inner circle allowed them access to, and use of, such luxury goods as alcohol and tobacco, as well as other rare supplies and delicacies.

Being single women, most became wealthy and prosperous in a society where such things would have been nearly impossible otherwise.

These women warriors were openly feared and venerated in the Dahomean culture. Each was assigned slaves, including a young girl who would walk in front of her ringing a warning bell whenever her mistress left the king's palace. This would alert every male to clear a path for the revered warrior. Refusal to step aside and avert one's eyes led to severe consequences.

French colonial expansionism in the 1800s eventually resulted in an encroachment upon Dahomean territory, which, in turn, led to war. The Dahomeans fought several vicious battles against the French invaders, with the king's devoted women warriors always leading the charge. French officers frequently met horrific ends after being specifically targeted for slaughter by the Dahomey Amazons.

Over time, troop strength and superiority of French weaponry took its toll, and the final few battles between the two enemies saw the infamous Dahomean women warriors all but wiped out. The few legendary female African warriors who did survived the assault slowly assimilated into Dahomey society, with some eventually marrying and raising families. Other  Dahomey, devastated by the dissolution of their elite sisterhood, found life beyond their warrior culture extremely difficult. Regardless of their eventual fates, the remaining Dahomean women warriors evoked a high degree of respect, admiration, and fear from their fellow tribe members and all others who were aware of their fearsome reputation.

There is some disagreement as to when the last of the Dahomey Amazons died, but evidence suggests that some lived well into the mid-1900s, and that one actually lived beyond the age of one hundred, passing away in 1979.

# ACKNOWLEDGEMENTS

I'd like to give special "nods" to my dear mother who raised me (mostly right, I'd like to think), to my beautiful "warrior wife" who steers the ship, and to Jaynie Royal and the Regal House team for taking a chance on me and turning this long overdue concept into the book you're reading right now.